TAKING THE CROWN

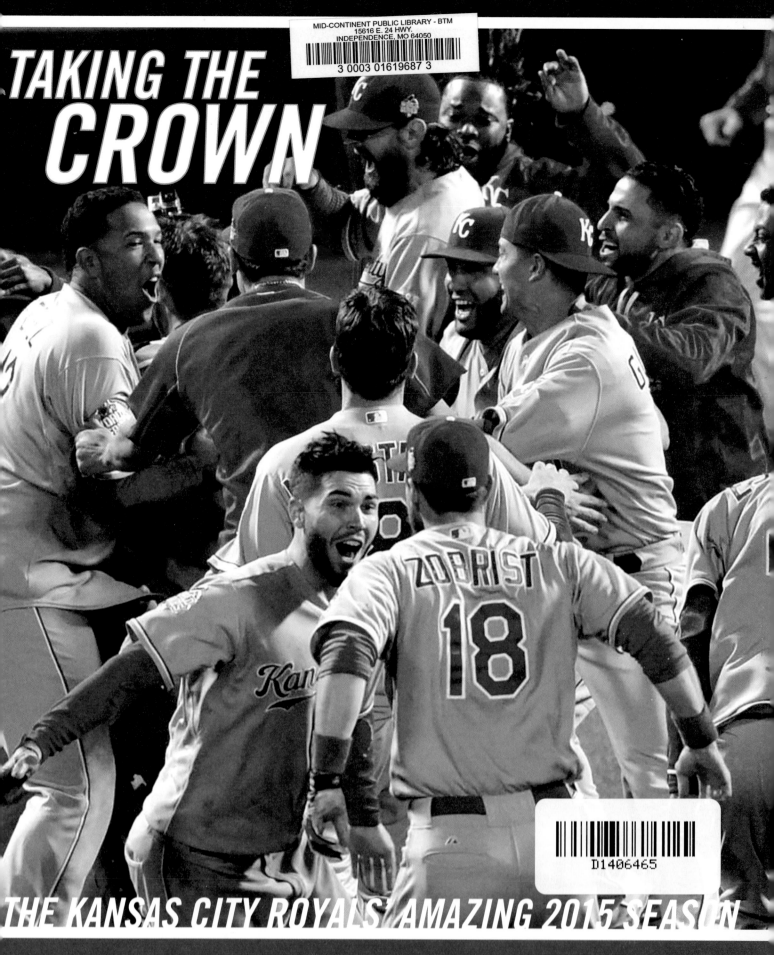

THE KANSAS CITY ROYALS' AMAZING 2015 SEASON

Contents

Foreword

By Dayton Moore

The joy and excitement of winning a World Series is difficult to put into words.

How do you describe the perseverance and the never-die attitude shown by our players? Or the positive attitude and complete trust that manager Ned Yost has in his players and coaches, and puts on display for them? Or the incredible love shown by our fans in Kansas City and around the world? It's tough to do.

Our goal, beginning with the final out of Game 7 of the 2014 World Series, was to win the 2015 World Series. All 30 major league teams have that goal each spring, but with how close we came a year ago, 90 feet from tying Game 7 in the ninth inning, winning in 2015 was not only a goal for the Kansas City Royals; it was an expectation.

The decisions we made in the offseason—signing players such as Kendrys Morales, Edinson Volquez, Alex Rios, Ryan Madson, Kris Medlen, and Chris Young, for instance—were made because we felt they would put us in a better position to win the World Series. Acquiring Johnny Cueto and Ben Zobrist through trades in July were critical for us to win the World Series. Because, ultimately, it comes down to the players.

And what a group of men we had in 2015. They embodied the term TEAM. They have tremendous character and they were more concerned about the team than they were personal accomplishments. In the clubhouse and on the field, they were a family. When we had key injuries during the 2015 season to Alex Rios, Omar Infante, Alex Gordon, Jason Vargas, and Greg Holland, people outside the organization wondered if the team could weather those losses. Their teammates stepped up. When Mike Moustakas, Chris Young, and Edinson Volquez each lost a parent throughout the season, the other players hurt with them but they lifted those three men up. Even when a player made an error on the field or a pitcher gave up a home run at a seemingly critical time, they all rallied together. I've been a part of close-knit teams before, but this group of Royals was special.

This has been a historic season in Royals baseball, and a large part of that is directly related to you as fans. More than 2.7 million fans attended games at Kauffman Stadium this year, which is the most ever for the Royals organization. I've said this before, but when I first took the job with the Royals, I noticed a large number of young fans walking into the stadium wearing T-shirts and jerseys from teams such as the Red Sox, Yankees, and Phillies. We wanted to create a culture that made kids want to wear blue shirts with names on the back like Gordon, Hosmer, Moustakas, and Perez. You and your children and grandchildren

Jarrod Dyson, who scored the go-ahead run in the 12th inning, holds the World Series trophy aloft.

have embraced our players. You've helped make Kauffman Stadium an electric sea of blue, and, believe me, our players feel that. You gave our team the best home-field advantage in the major leagues. For the way you've loved our team and the excitement you've shown not only at games but around Kansas City, thank you!

It will be awhile for the joy of this season to wear off for all of us. Once it does, I hope you'll enjoy reliving this 2015 World Series championship through the images and stories on the following pages. I'm sure I will. ∎

— *Dayton Moore*

Above: Eric Hosmer (center), Mike Moustakas, and Kendrys Morales are pumped after the first baseman scores the tying run in the ninth inning. Opposite: The large Kansas City contingent that occupied Citi Field celebrates with Jarrod Dyson.

World SERIES

After Wade Davis records the final out of Game 5, his Royals teammates rush onto the field.

WORLD SERIES: GAME 1

OCTOBER 27, 2015 | **ROYALS 5, METS 4 (14 INNINGS)**

New York Marathon

Royals Outlast Mets in Dramatic Game 1 Victory

If Game 1 was any indication, this is going to be a long, dramatic, and spectacular World Series.

It took more than five hours, 14 innings, an inside-the-park home run, a pitcher who was throwing without knowing that his father had passed away a few hours before, and yet another Royals comeback on a homer by one of the team's cornerstones, for Kansas City to take the first game of the World Series, 5–4, in front of an electric crowd at Kauffman Stadium.

Edinson Volquez pitched a typical Edinson Volquez game, giving the Royals' offense a chance. Volquez gave up three runs and six hits in six innings. He was pitching, though, unaware that his father Daniel died earlier that day from heart complications at the age of 63. He came out of the game after the sixth, shortly before the Royals tied it at 3–3. That's when Volquez learned about his father.

He is the third Royals player to have a parent die during the season. Mike Moustakas' mother Connie lost a battle with cancer and Chris Young's father Charles died in September.

"Most guys didn't know. I found out in I think it was the 14th inning, right before we won the game," Alex Gordon said. "I was standing next to [manager Ned Yost] and he told me. He said, 'Let's win this game for Volquez.'

"In the locker room during the celebration we all talked about it. That's tough. But we're a family, and we rallied around him and picked him up."

The teams were tied at 3–3 until the top of the eighth inning, when Kelvin Herrera gave up a two-out single to Juan Lagares, who stole second on the first pitch to Wilmer Flores. Then, uncharacteristic of the Royals during this postseason, Gold Glove first baseman Eric Hosmer misplayed a ball grounded by Flores. The error brought in Lagares and broke the tie.

With their backs against the wall, the Royals did what they did best in the playoffs—make a comeback. Mets manager Terry Collins turned to his closer, Jeurys Familia, who had 43 saves during the regular season with a 1.85 ERA. He hadn't blown a save since July 30, and he'd given up only two hits in 10 postseason innings. With one out, though, Alex Gordon, one of the cornerstones in general manager Dayton Moore's building plan for this organization, launched a monstrous 438-foot home run to straightaway center.

"He doesn't give up home runs, so we were all shocked by it," said Collins. "We liked where we were at."

After neither team scored in the 10th and 11th innings, Royals manager Ned Yost brought in Chris Young, who was scheduled to start Game 4, to pitch the 12th. Young was lights out. He faced nine batters and retired nine.

"It was a great sign by Dayton Moore late in the spring," Yost said of Young. "He's pitched so well for us

Just hours after his father had passed away, Edinson Volquez pitches during Game 1 of the World Series.

all year long in any role we've asked him to do. The thing that's so special to me is the confidence we all have in him. For him to go out and pitch the way that he does under any circumstance has just been a big lift to us all."

Alcides Escobar led off the bottom of the 14th by reaching on an error by Mets third baseman David Wright. The Royals took advantage. Ben Zobrist singled and pitcher Bartolo Colon intentionally walked Lorenzo Cain. Hosmer lifted a 2–2 pitch to deep right field, which allowed Escobar to tag from third, giving the Royals the win.

"Obviously, I wanted to redeem myself for what happened earlier," Hosmer said. "That's the beauty of this game, you always get a chance to redeem yourself. I just can't thank my teammates enough, [Gordon], and everybody picking me up right there and giving me another opportunity."

Coincidentally, Escobar scored the game's first run. The hype leading into the series was about the invasion of New York's "Fab Four" starting rotation—Matt Harvey, Jacob deGrom, Noah Syndergaard, and Steven Matz. It was enough that it could've left the Royals feeling like Elvis when the last "Fab Four" invaded New York. Much like Elvis, then, Escobar showed immediately that the Royals weren't going to worry about the hype, at least not against Harvey, the Game 1 starter.

Escobar, who's become known throughout this postseason for swinging at the first pitch with great results, got the greatest result possible in Game 1, as he drove Harvey's offering to deep left center. The ball landed between the left fielder Michael Conforto and center fielder Yoenis Cespedes and then went off Cespedes' foot. By the time the ball got back to the infield, Escobar had crossed home plate with an inside-the-park home run.

The win marks the first time in four attempts that the Royals have won Game 1 of a World Series.

"Two things you don't want in Game 1 of the World Series: one is to go 14 innings and the other is to lose," Yost said. "To find a way to grind that way out against a great team, both teams were matching pitch for pitch. We had opportunities, they'd make big pitches and get out of innings. But to grind through that game and to win it in the 14th inning was big." ■

Royals players celebrate after Alcides Escobar scores on a sacrifice fly by Eric Hosmer during the 14th inning of Game 1.

WORLD SERIES: GAME 2
OCTOBER 28, 2015 | ROYALS 7, METS 1

Cueto's K.C. Masterpiece

He's the First AL Pitcher to Throw Complete Game in World Series Since 1991

It would be difficult to find a Royals pitcher to match Johnny Cueto's performance in Game 5 of the ALDS against the Houston Astros, when he gave up two hits and two runs in eight innings. But, of course, Cueto matched, and perhaps, surpassed his ALDS outing with a complete-game, two-hitter against the New York Mets in Game 2 of the World Series. The win gives the Royals a two games to none lead in the series.

With the exception of one shaky inning, Cueto was brilliant in a game that the Royals won 7–1, beating the Mets' nearly unbeatable Jacob deGrom in the process.

"Tonight was everything we expected Johnny to be," said Royals manager Ned Yost. "He was on the attack. He kept the ball down. He changed speeds. It was just a spectacular performance by him."

After allowing only one base runner through the first three innings, Cueto gave up two walks in the fourth—a leadoff pass to Curtis Granderson and then one with one out to Daniel Murphy. And then after Yoenis Cespedes reached on a fielder's choice, Lucas Duda blooped an RBI single to left that scored Murphy and gave the Mets a 1–0 advantage. It was Duda's second hit of the game and last that Cueto would give up.

For the first four innings, deGrom, a young fireballer who won 14 games and had a 2.54 ERA and 205 strikeouts in 191 innings during the regular season, baffled Kansas City hitters. DeGrom retired the first seven Royals until walking Alex Gordon with one out in the third. But the Royals, as they've been known to do against top pitchers, broke through during the middle innings.

In the fifth inning, Gordon led off with his second walk of the night followed by back-to-back singles for Alex Rios and Alcides Escobar, the latter of which scored Gordon and tied the game at 1–1. After Ben Zobrist moved Rios and Escobar to second and third, respectively, and Lorenzo Cain lined out to center field, Eric Hosmer grounded a two-run base hit up the middle that gave the Royals a 3–1 lead. Kansas City added to its lead later in the inning when Mike Moustakas got a base hit that scored Hosmer. All told, the Royals sent nine to the plate in the inning against deGrom.

Cueto, meanwhile, continued to show the dominance Royals fans expected to see with every start. Starting with the final out of the run-scoring fourth inning, Cueto retired 13 straight Mets batters through the eighth inning.

Johnny Cueto celebrates after his masterful Game 2 start in which he gave up only two hits.

After the eighth Cueto pleaded with Yost to let him go back out. Yost told Cueto that Wade Davis was going to go out for the save, "but keep your head in the game because if we score a couple runs, I'm going to let you go back out."

Well, the Royals did just that. The first three batters reached for Kansas City against reliever Jon Niese. Moustakas started with a grounder to right field that went under the glove of a diving Duda. Salvador Perez then doubled down the left-field line. With runners at second and third, Gordon got a two-run double in shallow left that rolled slowly away from shortstop Wilmer Flores, scoring Moustakas. A deep sacrifice fly by Paulo Orlando and a two-out triple to dead center by Escobar gave the Royals three runs in the inning and a 7–1 lead.

The Royals, Hosmer said, knew Yost's deal with Cueto, and they wanted to scratch across two more runs.

"The offense and all the boys in the dugout really wanted to see him go back out," Hosmer said, "so I'm glad we could put up those runs so he could go back out and finish the job."

And finish it he did. Cueto induced ground-outs by the top two hitters in the New York lineup—Granderson and David Wright—giving him 15 consecutive outs, before walking Murphy. Cespedes, though, flied out to Orlando in right on a 2–0 count, giving Cueto the first complete game by an American League pitcher in the World Series since Jack Morris went the distance for the Minnesota Twins against the Atlanta Braves in Game 7 of the 1991 series.

"You saw it even in the last inning—still changing speeds, throwing strikes, using his change-up, pitching to both sides of the plate," said Mets manager Terry Collins. "We've just got to worry about making some adjustments in our lineup to start getting some hits. He's good. That's why they got him."

With his ALDS Game 5 outing and now Game 2 of the World Series, Cueto, who's the first pitcher from the Dominican Republic to throw a complete game in the World Series, is the only Royals pitcher to go at least eight innings in a postseason game since Bret Saberhagen threw a complete game against the St. Louis Cardinals in Game 7 of the 1985 World Series. ■

Johnny Cueto throws during the first inning of his 122-pitch, complete-game performance in the World Series.

WORLD SERIES: GAME 3
OCTOBER 30, 2015 | METS 9, ROYALS 3

Thor Throws Down the Hammer

Mets' Syndergaard Pitches with Authority, Silences Royals

There's a great scene in the movie *Bull Durham,* when Ebby Calvin "Nuke" LaLoosh gets in his catcher Crash Davis' face and says, "I wanna announce my presence with authority."

Mets pitcher Noah Syndergaard wasn't born when *Bull Durham* came out in 1988, but that's essentially what he did with his catcher Travis d'Arnaud when discussing their strategy against leadoff hitter Alcides Escobar. The plan nearly backfired as the Royals took an early lead in Game 3 at Citi Field, but the contest turned into all Mets as New York won 9–3, winning its first game of this World Series.

Escobar, who had an inside-the-park home run on the first pitch in Game 1 against Matt Harvey and then flied out to center field on the first pitch of Game 2 against Jacob deGrom, was ready to take a hack against Syndergaard, when the 98-mph fastball went sailing way high and inside, sending Escobar to the ground. After watching the second pitch, a curveball, cross for a strike, Escobar eventually struck out on a foul tip.

"I didn't like it at all. He even said he had a plan," Escobar said, referring to how Syndergaard pointed out in interviews before the game that he had something up his sleeve. "I feel like if that's the plan, it's a stupid plan. That's it. I don't think any pitcher is going to throw a ball at someone's head at 98 mph on the first pitch of the game. If he wants to do that, throw it at my feet, throw it anywhere, but not at my head."

Syndergaard's plan worked for the moment, as it kept Escobar off balance, but it fired up the rest of the Royals. Kansas City took a 1–0 lead when Eric Hosmer grounded out, scoring Ben Zobrist, who doubled and then went to third on a hit by Lorenzo Cain.

The lead was short-lived, though, as Kansas City starter Yordano Ventura gave up a two-run homer to David Wright with no outs in the bottom of the first.

The Royals came right back in the second and appeared to rattle Syndergaard with three consecutive singles by Salvador Perez, Alex Gordon, and Alex Rios, whose hit scored Perez but Gordon was thrown out—after a challenge play—at third base. Following a perfect sacrifice bunt by Ventura that moved Rios to third, Rios scored on a ball that got by d'Arnaud and went to the wall. For Royals fans it's too bad he scored that way because Escobar then singled off Syndergaard on the second pitch.

Syndergaard settled down after that, though, and went six innings en route to the win.

Noah Syndergaard sets the tone by throwing high and hard at Alcides Escobar, a tactic many deemed as dirty.

The Mets took the lead in the bottom of the third and didn't look back. Ventura, who didn't seem to have his best stuff, gave up a leadoff single to Syndergaard in the inning before Curtis Granderson came up and lined a homer to right that gave New York a 4–3 lead.

New York put the game out of reach—at least on this night—with a four-run sixth inning. Two of the runs came after a mental mistake by relief pitcher Franklin Morales, who was seeing his first inning of work in the World Series. With one out and one run across in the inning, the Mets had runners at first and third, the slower of the two being Juan Uribe at first. Granderson grounded the ball back to Morales, who turned to second but instead of throwing for a possible double play, he turned toward home, and then turned back toward second, making a wild throw past the bag. Everybody was safe. With the bases loaded, manager Ned Yost brought in Kelvin Herrera, who gave up an RBI single to Wright and a sacrifice fly to Yoenis Cespedes, which gave the Mets a 9–3 lead.

"That was a big out that we needed to get at that point," Yost said. "It was a ground ball right back to him. And his instincts were right, he was going to turnaround and fire to second. And again, I haven't talked to Salvy [catcher Salvador Perez], but Franklin said he heard Salvy say "home." So he stopped and turned and it was a mess from that point."

Morales' mental lapse was the second by a Kansas City pitcher in the game. In the fourth inning, with runners at second and third, Eric Hosmer fielded a grounder by Michael Conforto, but Ventura didn't cover the base, resulting in an RBI single for Conforto.

"My instincts were to watch the ball to see what Hoz was going to do," Ventura said through interpreter Christian Colon. "I just got caught watching the play."

The Royals lead the series now, two games to one, with two more to play at Citi Field. Although Syndergaard had a plan for one batter, the Royals have something bigger in mind.

"We have to forget about this," Escobar said. "The plan in here is to win." ■

Ben Zobrist receives a fist bump after scoring the first run of Game 3.

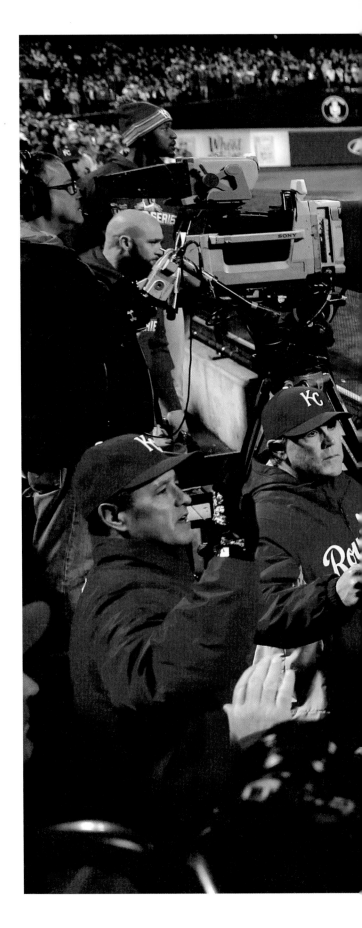

WORLD SERIES: GAME 4

OCTOBER 31, 2015 | ROYALS 5, METS 3

Trick and Treat

Royals Capitalize on Murphy Error to Launch Another Comeback

"I don't think it's overstating it when you say the World Series is on the line right here. If the Royals pull this one out of the fire, they are in great shape. This could be the crossroads of the 2015 World Series."

That was Denny Matthews' call seconds before Eric Hosmer tapped a slow grounder that went under the glove of Mets second baseman Daniel Murphy in a Bill Buckner-esque moment and allowed Ben Zobrist to score the tying run in the eighth inning, as the Royals went on to score twice more and stun the Citi Field crowd in a 5–3 win. The victory gives Kansas City a three game to one lead in the series.

Any listener to a Royals radio broadcast knows how much Matthews preaches a doomsday sermon for a team that allows late-inning walks and errors. That proved to be true for the Mets in the eighth inning on Halloween night. The game seemed to be set up perfectly for New York to tie the series, as the Mets held a 3–2 lead with their set-up reliever, Tyler Clippard, and closer, Jeurys Familia, rested and ready to go.

After retiring Alcides Escobar on a comebacker to the mound for the first out of the eighth, however, Clippard then issued back-to-back walks to Zobrist and Lorenzo Cain. Mets manager Terry Collins wasted no time going to Familia in hopes of closing the door on the Royals. Instead, Hosmer tapped the second pitch he saw toward Murphy, who didn't get down on the ball and it rolled to shallow right field. The error, which was reminiscent of Buckner's infamous error for Boston against the Mets at old Shea Stadium in 1986, allowed Zobrist to tie the game and moved Cain to third.

"I tried to one-hand it," Murphy said. "I just misplayed it. It went right under my glove. They made us pay for it. It put us in a really bad spot, and that's frustrating."

Familia then gave up back-to-back RBI singles to Mike Moustakas and Salvador Perez—his third hit of the game—that brought in Cain and Hosmer. So, to Matthews' constant point, the two walks and error all scored for the Royals, giving Kansas City a 5–3 lead.

"It's a team that looks for just a little crack," manager Ned Yost said of his Royals. "If they find a little crack, they're going to make something happen. It's amazing the way that they do that, and they do it in a number of different ways. The most important thing is that they put the ball in play. They make things happen by putting the ball in play. It's just a phenomenal group."

Wade Davis came in for Kansas City in the bottom of the eighth, searching for a six-out save. Davis had no problem retiring the Mets in order in the eighth, but then made things interesting in the ninth. After Davis struck out David Wright leading off the ninth, he then gave up consecutive singles to Murphy and Yoenis Cespedes. With runners at first and second, Lucas Duda lined an 0–1 pitch

Salvador Perez reacts after hitting an RBI single—his third hit of the game—in the eighth inning.

to Moustakas, who fired across the diamond to Hosmer, doubling off Cespedes. It was Davis' first save of the World Series.

"We feel like, if we can keep the game close until the later innings, we're going to win it," Yost said, "because our bullpen is so dynamic they give us a chance to win those type of games."

Kansas City starting pitcher Chris Young didn't factor into the decision, but he pitched well enough for the win (albeit not long enough). Young allowed two runs on two hits and one walk in four innings. Although Michael Conforto hit one of his two home runs of the night off Young (the other was against Danny Duffy), the second run charged to Young was one of the few mental lapses Kansas City's defense has displayed in the first two games played at Citi Field.

Following mental mistakes by Yordano Ventura and Franklin Morales in Game 3, the Mets added their second run of Game 4 Saturday night on a sacrifice fly to Alex Rios for the second out. It scored Wilmer Flores. Only problem is that Rios thought it was the third out of the inning, and he jogged a few steps toward the dugout before realizing it was the third out and throwing the ball toward home plate. Flores scored easily.

The Royals cut New York's lead to 2–1 in the top of the fifth against starter Steven Matz on an RBI single by Alex Gordon that scored Perez from third, but the Mets came right back in the bottom of the inning and made it 3–1 on Conforto's second home run.

Kansas City cut into the Mets lead one more time before the eighth-inning rally, when Cain had a base hit to center in the sixth that scored Zobrist.

With the win, the Royals have set a major-league record by winning six games this postseason when they've trailed by multiple runs. It's their seventh overall come-from-behind win during this postseason. How do they do it?

"It's experience, it's character, you know, it's a group of really, really talented players," Yost said. "A lot of it is a mind-set. We're on the biggest stage that you can play in front of and these guys are totally confident in their abilities. They're cool as cucumbers. They never panic because they've been through it before and they know they're capable of doing it again, and it's something that they believe in their heart that they can accomplish. It's fun to sit there and be the manager of that group." ∎

Alex Gordon rips an RBI single to deep right field to give Kansas City its first run in Game 4.

Comeback Kids Are Kings

Royals Outlast Harvey, Finish Off Mets in 12th to Take the Crown

Fitting. The comeback kids did it again for a second consecutive night. Only this time it was for the world championship, as the Kansas City Royals overcame a two-run deficit at Citi Field in the ninth inning and went on to beat the New York Mets, 7–2, in 12 innings in Game 5, becoming the 2015 World Series champs.

It's the first world championship for the Royals since 1985. Unlike 1985's 11–0 win in Game 7, the decisive game in 2015 had a little more nail biting before the Royals took the crown.

One night after getting shell-shocked by another Royals late comeback, the Mets needed a big outing from ace Matt Harvey to extend the series. Harvey did not disappoint. For eight innings he delivered one of the top performances of the postseason, striking out nine through eight shutout innings.

Heading into the ninth, when Harvey learned that manager Terry Collins was going to bring in New York's closer, Jeurys Familia, to finish the game, Harvey pleaded with Collins to leave him in.

"[Harvey] came over and said, 'I want this game. I want it bad. You've got to leave me in,'" Collins said after the game. "He said, 'I want this game in the worst way.' So obviously, I let my heart get in the way of my gut."

"It didn't work," Collins added. "It's my fault."

No one could blame Collins for sticking with Harvey. Although Harvey threw his 100th pitch in the eighth inning, the Royals weren't getting good swings. Harvey, who started Game 1 but didn't factor into the decision, allowed only four hits—all singles—and walked one through eight innings in Game 5.

But the ninth was a different story, especially against this resilient, never-say-die bunch of Royals.

With the Royals trailing 2–0, Lorenzo Cain worked a full-count walk and then Harvey gave up an opposite-field double to Eric Hosmer, scoring Cain. That ended Harvey's night, as Collins went to Familia, who had blown a save opportunity about 24 hours earlier.

Familia got Mike Moustakas to ground out to first baseman Lucas Duda for the first out, but it advanced Hosmer to third base. Salvador Perez, who popped out for the final out of the World Series in Game 7 in 2014, rolled a soft grounder toward short. Third baseman David Wright fielded the ball, checked Hosmer, and threw to first for the second out. However, as soon as Wright threw it, Hosmer broke for home. He slid headfirst across home plate for the tying run as Duda's throw sailed past catcher Travis d'Arnaud.

With Hosmer's gutsy baserunning, Familia had recorded his third blown save in a World Series, which hadn't happened since 1969.

"We never quit. We never put our heads down," said Perez, who was selected as the World Series MVP.

A savvy base runner, Eric Hosmer celebrates after scoring the tying run in the ninth inning.

"We always compete to the last out."

Perez helped the Royals get to that last out by leading off the 12th with a single against Addison Reed. Jarrod Dyson came in as a pinch-runner and stole second as the clock passed midnight in New York. After Alex Gordon's groundout moved Dyson to third, manager Ned Yost called on Christian Colon to pinch-hit for pitcher Luke Hochevar. Colon, who scored the winning run in the 2014 wild-card game against Oakland, had not played in this postseason. But the long break didn't affect him as he singled to left and gave the Royals their first lead of the game at 3–2.

The Royals kept the line going, though. Paulo Orlando reached on an error by Daniel Murphy, whose error in Game 4 started Kansas City's rally. Alcides Escobar doubled home Colon, making it 4–2. After Ben Zobrist was intentionally walked to load the bases with one out, Cain greeted relief pitcher Bartolo Colon with a bases-clearing double, giving Kansas City five runs in the inning, the most by a team in extra innings in World Series history.

Not taking any chances with a 7–2 lead, Yost brought in Wade Davis to close the game. Davis was the fourth Royals pitcher, after Kelvin Herrera and Hochevar, who got the win. Davis, who threw two innings for the save Saturday night, wasted little time in striking out Duda and d'Arnaud, putting the Royals one out from a championship.

Michael Conforto singled, but then Davis finished striking out the side by catching Wilmer Flores looking. Davis tossed his glove in the air and awaited backup catcher Drew Butera, commencing the celebration on the field. Fittingly, the clincher was the Royals' seventh comeback of the 2015 postseason after trailing by at least two runs.

"I couldn't have written a better script," Yost said.

The Mets jumped on Kansas City starter Edinson Volquez in the first inning on a leadoff home run by Curtis Granderson. It was the second time Volquez gave up a homer to Granderson, who hit one in the fifth inning of Game 1.

Granderson scored New York's second run of the game in an inning that could've been disastrous for the Royals. Volquez walked Granderson leading off the sixth inning before giving up a base hit to David Wright. Murphy then reached on an error on a grounder to first that bounced off Hosmer's glove and loaded the bases with no outs. After Yoenis Cespedes popped out to Escobar for the first out, Duda lifted a deep sacrifice fly that scored Granderson and gave the Mets a 2–0 lead. Volquez avoided any more trouble by inducing a groundout by Travis d'Arnaud, ending the inning.

Volquez, who rejoined the team a day earlier following the death of his father in the Dominican Republic, gave up two runs and two hits in six innings. He also walked five and struck out five. As solid as he was on the mound, Volquez went into the Royals history book for something he did at the plate. Volquez led off the top of the third with a single to right against Harvey. That's the first time a Royals pitcher has recorded a hit in a World Series game.

And, for the first time in 30 years, the Royals were World Series champions.

"To be able to win this is very, very special, with this group of guys," said Yost. "With their character, with their heart, with their passion, with the energy that they bring every single day, I mean, they leave everything on the field." ■

The Royals pose with the World Series trophy at Citi Field after winning their first World Series in 30 years.

Perez Named World Series MVP

One Year After Popping Out to End Game 7, Catcher Leads Royals to Title

Salvador Perez always seems to have a smile on his face. That smile was even bigger as he was announced as the World Series MVP to the whooping and hollering of his teammates in the Kansas City clubhouse at Citi Field after the Royals beat the Mets 7–2 in Game 5 of the 2015 World Series.

Perez batted .364 (8-for-22) with two doubles, two RBIs, and three runs scored during the World Series. He had three hits in Game 4, including an RBI single as part of Kansas City's three-run eighth inning. In the clinching Game 5, Perez had only one hit, but it was a big one: the leadoff single in the 12th that, on the legs of pinch runner Jarrod Dyson, turned into the game-winning run. And, it was on Perez's groundout in the ninth inning that Eric Hosmer scored the tying run that sent the game into extra innings.

Behind the plate, Perez was a workhorse. After Sunday's game, he'd caught 2,721 regular-season and postseason innings in 2014 and '15. As important as his ability as a catcher, though, Perez embodies general manager Dayton Moore's plan for players to come up through the farm system together, join the established Royals and some extra puzzle pieces in Kansas City, and win a championship together. Perez, whom the Royals signed out of Venezuela when he was 16, was a big part of that building process.

"I always say we feel like a family here," Perez said after Game 5. "We've got the same group, almost the same group, as when I played my first year in 2007 in Arizona, the Rookie League. It's amazing to now win a World Series and see the same guys with you."

Perez was asked after the game if the disappointment of popping out for the final out of the 2014 World Series outweighed the excitement he was feeling as a World Series champion.

In typical Perez fashion, he got a wide grin as he answered: "Kansas City is No. 1. Who cares about what happened last year?" ■

The always ebullient Salvador Perez receives the World Series MVP trophy after hitting .364 in the series.

The Royals take batting practice prior to their Opening Day game against the Chicago White Sox at Kauffman Stadium on April 6.

Road To The
TITLE

America's Team Becomes America's Most Wanted

Early Season Skirmishes Reveal Different Side of Royals

Rocky Balboa was never the villain. The Cinderella? Sure, at some point in the first four installments of Rocky. But never the villain—unless you count him as a villain for making Rocky V. Frankly, it's really tough to go from Cinderella to villain.

Yet, in terms of a baseball season, it took about one month of games for the Royals to go from America's Darlings October 2014—unless you lived in California or Baltimore—in to the new "Nasty Boys" in April 2015.

It started innocently enough during the Royals' first roadtrip of the year to Anaheim. Yordano Ventura, making his second start of the season, gave up a one-out base hit to Mike Trout in the sixth inning with the Royals leading 7–1. Albert Pujols doubled, scoring Trout, who slid at home plate. As Trout got up, Ventura, who was backing up home plate, started jawing with the Angels' All-Star.

"I just got a base hit, I got to first base and he was staring at me," Trout said after the game. "I didn't think I did anything wrong—and then he got in my face. I'm not trying to get in any fights or anything, and I'm just trying to play baseball."

Shortly after that incident, Ventura complained about a cramp in his calf, and he left the game. It was the second time in as many starts that Ventura, who

signed a five-year contract before the season, left the game early because of a physical ailment. On Opening Day, he left early because of a thumb cramp.

America's Darlings really began to gain a new identity during the first home series after the incident in Anaheim, when the Royals played host to Oakland, the team it beat in the 2014 wild-card game.

In the first game of the three-game set, in something that looked more akin to Royals–A's circa 1976, Oakland's Brett Lawrie slid late into second base to break up a possible double play. He went past the bag and took out shortstop Alcides Escobar, who ended up being diagnosed with a sprained knee. The play caused both benches to clear.

The next day, immediately after Josh Reddick tagged Ventura for a three-run homer, Ventura plunked Lawrie with a pitch. Some would call it a "good old-fashioned baseball" move. The A's didn't appreciate it, though, and the benches cleared. Ventura was ejected.

In Sunday's series finale, the benches cleared yet again. This time, there was Lorenzo Cain getting hit on the knee by a pitch by Scott Kazmir, and Kelvin Herrera throwing a 100-mph fastball behind Lawrie. In all, five Royals were ejected, including Herrera.

"I don't mean to hurt anybody," he said after-

Umpire Greg Gipson ejects Royals manager Ned Yost during the first inning of the Royals' home game against the Athletics on April 19. Yost and Royals pitching coach Dave Eiland were ejected in the first inning after Lorenzo Cain was hit by a pitch from Oakland's Scott Kazmir.

wards. "I was just trying to throw inside, but just a bad grip on that fastball. It started raining pretty good. And they just tossed me out of the game."

If only that were the end of it for the Royals. Ventura and his mates were involved in yet another bench clearing only four days after the Oakland finale. This time, in Chicago, it got a little uglier. In the seventh inning, Ventura fielded a soft grounder off the bat of Adam Eaton. The two players stared each other down and exchanged words before Ventura threw to first for the out. The benches cleared and punches were thrown. Ventura was ejected for a second consecutive start.

Four others were ejected, including White Sox pitcher Jeff Samardzija, who threw a punch that connected with Mike Jirschele and sent the Royals' third-base coach down to the ground.

"I don't think they're punks," Eaton said of the Royals to ESPN. "I don't believe that for a second. They're a bunch of young guys who are very, very good. I think they're trying to find their identity."

Unfortunately, that identity had gone from a great story of a bunch of young, ego-less, hungry players, to the new bruiser on the block.

"We're not a group of guys that are looking to start any scuffles," Eric Hosmer told ESPN. "We just want to go out and play baseball. We don't want to get disrespected out there, and we're going to stick up for each other."

In spite of the early-season brawls and beanballs and ejections and suspensions, Royals pitchers were in the bottom half of hitting batters in all of Major League Baseball. Out of 30 teams, the Royals were 16th on the list with hitting 52 batters during the 2015 regular season. Meanwhile, Royals hitters were plunked 77 times, which was third-most in the majors behind Pittsburgh (89) and Tampa (84).

Brett Lawrie's late slide into second base on April 17, spiking Royals shortstop Alcides Escobar and spraining Escobar's knee, caused both benches to clear.

As the season progressed, the villain image faded a little, only to flare up on a Sunday in August at Toronto. Josh Donaldson had hit two home runs earlier in the series, and Edinson Volquez plunked Donaldson on the arm in the first inning of the finale.

"He was pimping everything he does," Volquez said of Donaldson after the game. "Somebody hits you, you've got to take it, because you're pimping everything you do."

In the eighth, Toronto's Aaron Sanchez hit Escobar in the thigh with a pitch. Both benches cleared.

Knuckleballer R.A. Dickey viewed the situation and the Royals overall a little differently. "I think they're used to pushing people around," he said. "So when they come onto the playground and there's a kid that's bigger than they are for a day, I think it probably (ticks) them off. And I can't blame 'em."

To go along with the last part of Dickey's comment, the Royals were simply standing up for their teammates. It's the old playground game of "King of the Hill." Only, there was an incident in Game 3 of the World Series when young Mets starter Noah Syndergaard threw the first pitch of the game high and tight to Escobar. Royals detractors hailed it as "good, old-school baseball." After all, Escobar has been one of the hottest hitters in the postseason. Syndergaard went so far as to say he meant to throw the pitch high and inside.

"I feel like it really made a statement to start the game off," Syndergaard, who's nicknamed "Thor," said. He later added, "If they have a problem with me throwing inside, then they can meet me at 60 feet, six inches away. I've got no problem with that."

Funny, Syndergaard's words echoed the type of attitude that started all of this for the Royals in early 2015. Maybe there will be a new "villain" come 2016. ■

The Mets sent a message on the first pitch of Game 3 of the World Series. Noah Syndergaard's 98-mph fastball was high and tight, knocking Alcides Escobar to the ground.

New Faces Reach Big Places

Morales, Volquez, and Rios Exceed Expectations

The three names didn't exactly invoke excitement amongst the Royals faithful. After the Royals' first trip to the postseason in 29 years in 2014, the club did not re-sign James Shields, Billy Butler, or Nori Aoki. And the response to the off-season acquisitions signed to replace the departing stars in 2015—Edinson Volquez, Kendrys Morales, and Alex Rios—was less than ho-hum.

On the surface, the reaction might have been understandable. While Volquez, who signed for two years and $20 million, went 13–7 with a 3.04 ERA for Pittsburgh in 2014, Morales and Rios were both coming off less-than-stellar campaigns. Recovering from injury, Morales hit .218 with eight home runs and 42 RBIs for Seattle and Minnesota in 2014. He signed for two years and $17 million. Rios, who signed for one year and $11 million, was injured late in the 2014 season after hitting .280 in 131 games.

That didn't stop the criticism. One of the least critical came from Grantland.com: "Just like last winter, the Royals patched every fraying position. This time, though, the replacements aren't reassuring."

The column continued: "Even if everything comes up Kansas City, though, the new arrivals remain probable downgrades: Butler, Aoki, and Shields, who combined for 5.7 WAR last season, are projected to double the 2015 production of Morales, Rios, and Volquez, the players who replaced them."

"Double the production?" Hold that thought.

The negative response wasn't only from the media and bloggers. The *Kansas City Star* ran a reader poll asking what fans thought about the signings. Of the 1,195 people who responded, only nine percent thought the moves were "Great! These three acquisitions will put the Royals over the top in 2015." Sixty-seven percent said "Pretty good. Given their financial constraints, these were shrewd moves." The final 24 percent picked "Not a fan. These guys are mid-level additions. The Royals needed more."

The naysayers should be ashamed. Dayton Moore and his staff had the golden touch after all. All three acquisitions contributed to the success of the club either during the regular season, in the postseason, or both.

Volquez, taking over for Shields as a top-of-the-rotation starter, won 13 games for the Royals during the regular season. He led them to a Game 1 win in the ALCS against Toronto, and went six innings, allowing six hits and three runs against New York in Game 1 of the World Series. He did not factor into

Alex Rios celebrates at first base after singling in the fifth inning of the ALCS against the Blue Jays, one of Rios' former teams. Rios batted .368 in the series.

the decision. Sadly, moments after the game, Volquez found out that his father had died hours earlier.

Without question, the best signing of the 2014 offseason was Morales, who hadn't been the same since he broke his ankle in a freak accident in May 2010. Then with the Angels, Morales was celebrating a walk-off grand slam when he went into the dog pile of teammates at home plate and landed awkwardly. He didn't play in the majors again for 22 months. He had a slow spring in 2014 and subsequent disappointing year. But the Royals felt he could add an important piece.

"When we come up with the bases loaded or first and second, we need somebody who can be a presence, drive the ball in the alley and clear the bases," Moore said at the press conference announcing the signing of Morales.

Morales certainly became that presence. His offensive numbers from his first year with the Royals resembled his pre-injury 2009 season, when he was mentioned as an American League MVP candidate (he finished fifth). In 2009 he was .306/.355/.569 with 108 RBIs. In 2015 he was at .290/.362/.485 with 106 RBIs.

Rios was perhaps the least lucky in the group in 2015. In his first seven games with the Royals he hit .321 with an .809 on-base-plus-slugging percentage and drove in eight runs before being hit on the hand against Minnesota and heading to the disabled list. He missed about six weeks.

When Rios returned, he slogged through June and July, logging only as many RBIs as he had in the first seven games of the year. In that span his batting average was .243.

Through August and September, Rios played better, and his average during those months was .275. That timeframe did not pass uneventfully, however, as Rios and reliever Kelvin Herrera came down with chickenpox in early September.

In the postseason, however, Rios made up for lost time by knocking 12 hits—including two doubles and a home run—in the first 13 games. After a season in which fans often criticized his lack of production at the plate, Rios delivered in a number of key situations throughout the American League playoffs.

Returning to that "double the production" prediction mentioned in the Grantland.com piece in December 2014, that didn't exactly come to fruition. In fact, all of the "new" Royals matched or out-performed their predecessors in 2015 in one way or another.

Shields went 13–7 with a 3.91 ERA in 202⅓ innings for San Diego. Volquez was 13-9 with a 3.55 ERA in 200⅓ innings.

Butler hit .251 with 135 hits, 28 doubles, 15 home runs, 65 RBIs, and 63 runs scored for Oakland. Morales hit .290 with 165 hits, 41 doubles, 22 home runs, 106 RBIs, and 81 runs.

Aoki, playing for San Francisco, hit .287 with 102 hits, 12 doubles, five homers, 26 RBIs, and 42 runs. Rios batted .255 with 98 hits, 22 doubles, four home runs, 32 RBIs, and 40 runs. ■

Edinson Volquez throws during Game 1 of the World Series. Volquez won 13 games for the Royals in 2015.

A Bumpy Road to the Crown

Injuries, Illness Shaped Royals' Path to the Postseason

To those whose exposure to the Royals was limited to the World Series, Kansas City might have appeared to be a charmed team, destined to complete in 2015 what it failed to finish in 2014. Those who watched those final games but did not follow Kansas City throughout the season might well assume the Royals largely escaped the most common misfortune to befall a baseball team—injury.

That certainly was true of the 2014 club. The only major injury for the Royals in '14 happened during spring training, when pitcher Luke Hochevar hurt his elbow and was lost for the season after undergoing Tommy John surgery. In hindsight, by the '14 All-Star break it became clear that Hochevar's injury helped usher in the game's most dominant relief pitcher, Wade Davis, and the famous "HDH" at the back of the Kansas City bullpen.

The Royals weren't so lucky in 2015. Kansas City lost a number of players for significant stretches. Among the injured were right fielder Alex Rios, left fielder Alex Gordon, starting pitcher Jason Vargas, second baseman Omar Infante, and closer Greg Holland.

Rios, new to the team in 2015, was the first to see his season shaken up. In his first seven games, Rios cracked nine hits and knocked in eight. Then a pitch hit him and broke a bone in his left hand, knocking him out of the lineup for the rest of April and all but a single game in May. He was slow to come back, and didn't seem to be back to form until the postseason. To add illness to injury, at the end of the regular season Rios and reliever Kelvin Herrera both missed time when they came down with chickenpox.

The most significant of the 2015 injuries, in terms of being difficult to replace, was Gordon, the Platinum Glove winner who suffered a groin injury July 8. At the time of the injury, the left fielder had a batting average of .279 and an on-base percentage of .394. He had 11 home runs, 13 doubles, and had walked 39 times.

The Royals lost another contributor two weeks after Gordon's injury, when Vargas felt a pain in his elbow during his first start after coming off the disabled list after suffering a different injury. This would require season-ending Tommy John surgery. Vargas was 5–2 with a 3.98 ERA in nine starts in 2015.

To see Gordon and Vargas go down in quick succession was sobering.

"This team is usually a pretty healthy team," third baseman Mike Moustakas told the *Kansas City Star*. "To see Gordo go down the way he went down, and now for Vargy to go down, those are two key pieces

Alex Gordon strains his right groin while chasing down a fly ball against Tampa Bay on July 8. The injury sidelined the Royals' left fielder until September 1.

for this team. You hate to lose any one of those guys. But at the end of the day, we're going to have to go out and find a way to win a game without those guys."

Although there was understandable concern about what would happen to the Royals, particularly in Gordon's absence, the club somehow continued to win. While Gordon was out, the Royals went 31–17. Dyson and Paulo Orlando shared most of the left field duties until the club acquired Ben Zobrist from Oakland at the end of July. Zobrist, who became the club's everyday second baseman, started 18 games in left.

After nearly two months, Gordon returned to the lineup on September 1. Like Rios, Gordon did not regain his earlier form immediately upon his return. In fact, he had a batting average of .250 and an on-base percentage of .327 in his last 26 regular season games. But the Gordon of old showed up in the postseason, contributing several key hits, including a ninth-inning blast to center field at Kauffman Stadium that tied up Game 1 of the World Series, a game the Royals eventually won in 14 innings.

In late September, the Royals had to contend with the loss of two more key players. Second baseman Omar Infante was ruled out with an oblique strain. It had been a down year for Infante offensively, but he played solid defense, and he and shortstop Alcides Escobar had developed great chemistry on the middle infield.

The loss of Infante was allayed in part by the acquisition of the versatile Zobrist, who took on Infante's role at second base and provided an offensive upgrade at the position. In 59 regular-season games with Kansas City, Zobrist batted .284 with an on-base percentage of .364.

In addition to losing Infante in September, Kansas City had to shut down bullpen anchor Holland. The reliever helped take the Royals all the way to the World Series in 2014, but Holland had not been able to perform at the same level in 2015. Like Vargas, Holland would undergo Tommy John surgery. Holland revealed he had been playing injured for some time, but he felt he could still contribute, so he refused an MRI and continued. The Royals allowed him to do so until he was no longer giving the team what it needed on the mound.

"He's an unbelievable competitor," Royals general manager Dayton Moore told the *Star*. "He's a guy that you trust to pitch through those types of situations. And he's done an incredible job for us. He's done an incredible job for us this year."

So the Royals entered the 2015 postseason without their star closer, without their regular second baseman, without one of their starting pitchers, and with their perennial Gold Glove left fielder and starting right fielder still working to regain the rhythm they each had prior to suffering injuries.

For those who could not return to action, others stepped in. Those who did return found a way to contribute once again.

As the Royals earned seven of their first nine postseason victories by either coming from behind or regaining the lead, such resilience on the field could hardly be considered surprising. ◼

Greg Holland regroups on the mound during the Royals' win over the Cleveland Indians on September 15. The Royals' dominant closer during the team's 2014 season, Holland pitched with a torn ligament in his elbow for an extended period before the Royals shut him down in September 2015.

13
CATCHER

Salvador Perez

Perpetually Joyous Backstop Deftly Handles Pitchers, Provides Clutch At-Bats

If someone needed to find Salvador Perez but had never seen him, perhaps the best way to direct that person would be to instruct him to look for the Royals player who appeared to be having the most fun of anyone on the diamond.

As the Kansas City Royals chugged through the regular season toward what had been the stated goal all along—the World Series—their 25-year-old catcher Perez made the journey a conspicuously joyous one. After each game he would dump a bucket of Gatorade on whichever one of his teammates was standing for an on-field postgame interview.

When players started to try to avoid the beverage showers, Perez switched it up, idling without a bucket and attracting attention so that a teammate to whom he had delegated the dumping could accomplish the mission and keep the surprise intact.

Perez was rarely spotted without a wide grin. After many wins he responded with unrestrained enthusiasm, hollering in triumph and bounding out to meet his teammates with emphatic hugs and elaborate handshakes.

Behind home plate, however, Perez meant business and he did his job well in 2015, as he had in his two previous full seasons as catcher for the Royals. In July Perez, who turned 25 in May, was selected to his third All-Star Game and in October he was nominated for a third Gold Glove. That's after catching 150 games in 2014 and 142 in 2015.

"When it's all said and done, his reputation is going to be every bit as good as Pudge Rodriguez's is," manager Ned Yost told the the *Kansas City Star* in 2014. "Salvy's going to end up being one of the best catchers to come out of Latin America of all time."

Rodriguez, the 14-time All-Star and 13-time Gold Glove winner who was named the American League MVP in 1999, is not the only masterful catcher to whom Perez's performance has drawn comparisons.

Senior team advisor Bill Fischer gave general manager Dayton Moore a similarly dramatic report on Perez's ceiling after he watched Perez play in the Arizona Rookie League in 2007. "I've just seen the Latin Johnny Bench," Fischer said to Moore. And Fischer would know. He was the pitching coach for

Salvador Perez has some fun on the field at Kauffman Stadium during a workout before the 2015 World Series. The Royals' catcher was named to his third All-Star team in 2015.

Cincinnati Reds' "Big Red Machine" of the 1970s.

Although Bench was an offensive force for the Reds, Perez had not put up overly impressive batting statistics, finishing both the 2014 and 2015 seasons with a .260 average. He did have 21 home runs in 2015, improving upon the 17 the previous year.

Like many of the Royals, however, Perez had a knack for the clutch hit. He most notably knocked in the run that gave Kansas City its win in the wacky wild-card game in 2014 and he continued to deliver the following season.

With runners in scoring position in 2015, Perez had a .311 batting average. He had 138 hits in the regular season, and 42 of them came in such situations.

Of course, Perez performed so well behind the plate that whatever he did in the batter's box was merely as a bonus. As the Royals closed in on their second World Series in as many years, the 6'3", 230-pound Perez did it all while getting knocked around. Foul tips found him often, thanks mostly to his size, but he rarely left games.

Yost found a couple of occasions where he felt the need to take Perez out of games early, but Yost, a former catcher, knows the beating is part of the gig.

"But Sal is suited perfectly for it," Yost said. "He's a big guy, extremely tough and he can take a beating."

Part of that determination stems from a love for the game. Another part of it comes from an unmistakable affection for the other members of the organization.

"Everybody just feeds off his enthusiasm and energy that he brings to the ballpark every day," Yost said. "That's why I think all the players can unite behind Salvador knowing that he helps bring the energy every single day." ∎

Salvador Perez and closer Wade Davis celebrate after the Royals clinched their second consecutive pennant, defeating the Blue Jays in Game 6 of the 2015 ALCS.

Teammates have come to expect a Gatorade shower from Salvador Perez after a big win. Here he dumps a cooler on first baseman Eric Hosmer after the Royals' clinching Game 6 win over the Blue Jays in the ALCS.

35
FIRST BASE

Eric Hosmer

8
THIRD BASE

Mike Moustakas

Back-to-Back First-Round Picks Helped "Flip the Switch"

There are countless reasons why the Royals went to back-to-back World Series. After all, the 2014 and 2015 Royals embody the word "team" perhaps as well as any other current major sports team. But much of the success can be pointed back to a simple question in 2011: "When are we going to flip the switch?"

That was a question that Gene Watson, the Royals director of professional scouting, kept asking general manager Dayton Moore.

In not so many words, many Royals fans wondered the same thing. The Royals were coming off a 95-loss season in 2010, but they had a world of talent in the minor leagues, including the 2007 and 2008 first-round draft picks Mike Moustakas (second overall) and Eric Hosmer (third overall), respectively. Then were names such as Salvador Perez, Danny Duffy, and Kelvin Herrera.

No offense to those last three names, but there was more anticipation on the two first-round picks. Hosmer and Moustakas seemed to be the future of

the organization, the younger players who would help build the club around the likes of Alex Gordon and Billy Butler.

"They fit right in with what we're doing," manager Ned Yost said of Hosmer and Moustakas during spring training in 2011. "They're both quality kids in the clubhouse and outside the clubhouse. We know they're extremely talented, but their make-up is off the charts for kids their age. They're special kids."

Early in 2011 Hosmer was the first one who looked to be ready for a ticket to Kansas City. During the first month of the 2011 season he was leading all of the minors in batting average (.439) and on-base percentage (.525).

Moore received a call from Chino Cadahia, who joined the Royals as a special assistant in 2011, and Jack Maloof, who was one of the organization's hitting coaches. They started talking to him about Hosmer: "This guy is ready for the major leagues. What are you waiting for?"

A few weeks later on May 6, 2011, Hosmer made

Mike Moustakas (left) and Eric Hosmer (right) celebrate after combining to overpower the Toronto Blue Jays during the Royals' dominant 14-2 win in Game 4 of the American League Championship Series.

his major league debut against the Oakland A's. Although he went hitless in that game, he made a huge impact on that season. He went on to hit .293 with 19 home runs and 78 RBIs in 128 games.

Hosmer's fellow corner infielder, Moustakas, made his debut about a month later, on June 10 in Anaheim and singled off Angels (and future Royals pitcher) Ervin Santana for his first major league hit. Moustakas didn't get off to the same meteoric start as Hosmer, batting .182 in his first 53 games, through August 16. After that, though, things began to click. Moustakas had a 15-game hitting streak and batted .379 for the rest of the season.

In a perfect world, each player and their baseball-appropriate nicknames of "Hoz" and "Moose" would have kept rising from the 2011 season and put the Royals on their backs to reach the postseason in back-to-back seasons for the first time in three decades.

That's not exactly how it worked. Both players have had their share of struggles. After hitting 34 doubles, 20 home runs, and 73 RBIs in his first full season in Kansas City in 2012, Moustakas spent time at Triple A Omaha in 2014 as his batting average dipped to .212. Hosmer's average dropped to .232 with only 124 hits in 2012 and then nine home runs in 2014.

Appropriately, perhaps, each player had a coming out party, if you will, during the 2014 postseason. In fact, in back-to-back American League Division Series games against the Los Angeles Angels of Anaheim, "Hoz" and "Moose" propelled the Royals with a game-winning home run. In Game 1 at Anaheim, Moustakas, a California native, hit a solo homer in the 11th inning that gave the Royals a 3–2 lead. In Game 2 Hosmer hit a two-run homer in the 11th that put the Royals ahead 3–1.

"We came up and had similar paths, and it just made us better," Moustakas said after Game 2 of the 2014 ALDS. "Everything we went through in those minor leagues and even earlier in the season just made us better and got us ready for this situation."

Throughout the 2015 postseason, Hoz and Moose each came up with key hits and defensive plays as well. Look

Mike Moustakas watches Eric Hosmer take batting practice during spring training in 2012. The duo came up together, making their major league debuts about a month apart.

no further than Game 4 of the ALDS against the Houston Astros, when the Royals mounted a five-run rally in the eighth inning and avoided elimination.

Moustakas started everything, according to his teammates, with a rallying cry before the Royals came up to the plate in the eighth. During that inning Hosmer had an RBI single and then scored the tying run on a ground-out by Gordon. (Hosmer then iced the 9–6 win with a two-run homer in the ninth.)

Incidentally, besides Hosmer and Moustakas, the other three players made it to Kansas City in 2011. About 10 days after Hosmer's debut on May 18, Duffy pitched for the Royals. Two months after Moose came up, Perez saw action for the first time for the Royals on August 10. Herrera made his debut as a September call-up on the 21st of that month. ■

Above: Eric Hosmer, a 2008 first-round draft pick by the Royals, congratulates Mike Moustakas, a 2007 first-round draft pick, during a series in June of 2015. Opposite: Moustakas and Hosmer can rejoice after combining for three hits during the Royals' come-from-behind victory against the Houston Astros in Game 4 of the American League Division Series.

Going All In

Trades for Cueto and Zobrist Fortified World Series Run

Throughout their history, the Royals have never been what one might consider "great" at making trades near baseball's midseason deadline. They've tried; oh, they've tried. But sometimes bad decisions were made. Other times the economics dictated a move.

That's not to say all moves have been bad. In 2014, for instance, the club acquired Jason Frasor and Josh Willingham at the deadline in two separate deals. Both players were important for the club down the stretch and beyond.

But there have been very few times the Royals have been "all in" until this year when general manager Dayton Moore traded for ace pitcher Johnny Cueto and second baseman Ben Zobrist.

JULY 26

In one of the most talked about trades of the 2015 season, the Royals acquired Cueto from the Cincinnati Reds in exchange for minor league left-handed pitchers Brandon Finnegan, John Lamb, and Cody Reed.

"Johnny is going to a great situation there," Reds general manager Walt Jocketty said at the time of the trade. "He has people that he'll know. He's on a team that has a chance to go to the World Series."

Cueto, who won 20 games in 2014, was 7–6 with a 2.62 ERA in 19 starts at the time of the deal. The night before, Cueto threw eight scoreless innings against the Colorado Rockies in Denver.

Though it's unlike the Royals—at least throughout their history—to make this kind of move at the trade deadline, with a season-ending injury to starter Jason Vargas, the roller-coaster season for Yordano Ventura, and struggles by Jeremy Guthrie, their goal of winning the American League pennant and ultimately the World Series, was in some doubt. Never mind that the Royals were 58–38, which was on pace for 90 wins, and had a six-and-a-half-game lead in the division.

There's no telling how a trade will turn out. Who could've imagined that Wade Davis would turn into the most dominant closer in baseball when he was acquired as part of the deal that brought James Shields to Kansas City? Who would've guessed that the main two pieces of the Zack Greinke deal, Lorenzo Cain and Alcides Escobar, would be back-to-back American League Championship Series MVPs? The Cueto trade might've been riskier than those others because, for all intents and purposes, Cueto was a "rental."

He was a free agent after the season who'd be able to command a lot more money on the open market than Kansas City likely would be able to spend. And they were sending one pitcher with postseason experience

Acquired from the Cincinnati Reds on July 26, 2015, Johnny Cueto throws during his complete-game victory in Game 2 of the World Series.

in Finnegan and another in Lamb, who was 9–1 with a 2.67 ERA at Omaha at the time.

But this was the "new" Royals; the contending Royals under Moore say that if you dwell on what you're giving up in a trade, you'll never make the deal.

Cueto's first two starts were away from Kauffman Stadium in two hostile environments, Toronto and Detroit. Neither went exceptionally well. At Toronto on July 31, Cueto allowed seven hits, three runs, and two walks in six innings. The Royals lost 7–6. Five days later in Detroit, Cueto had a better outing with five hits, two walks, and two runs in seven innings, but Kansas City's offense struggled against Matt Boyd, and Cueto was tagged with the loss in the 2–1 final.

His first win in a Kansas City uniform came in the place where he'd end up being most comfortable: Kauffman Stadium. It was on August 10 against Detroit in a complete-game shutout, as he gave up only four hits, didn't allow a walk, and struck out eight. That would be his best performance until Game 2 of the World Series. In fact, Cueto struggled mightily throughout the rest of the regular season and into the postseason. He beat the Los Angeles Angels of Anaheim on August 15 but then lost his next five decisions and six out of seven. His regular season record with the Royals was 4–7.

Let's face it, though. The Royals didn't get Cueto for how he'd help during the regular season. So there wasn't a lot of panic.

"When pitchers go in slumps, it's a lot of things going wrong all at once," Yost said. "Sometimes he is making good pitches that are eight inches off the plate, and they're getting hit. Sometimes there are good pitches that become broken-bat hits or bloopers. It just happens. You get unlucky. I'd rather have it happen now than in October."

JULY 28

In case the Royals didn't indicate with their Cueto trade that they were trying to make a deep October/November run, two days later they acquired second baseman Ben Zobrist from the Oakland A's in exchange for minor league pitchers Sean Manaea and Aaron Brooks.

Zobrist, a switch-hitter, was batting .268 with six home runs. He was seen as someone who could fill in for Alex Gordon, who was out with a groin injury, or take over at second base.

"He's going to be great for us," Yost said at the time. "He's a really good run producer from both sides of the batter's box. He can play multiple positions. He gives us a lot of versatility. He's definitely got a winner's mentality."

In 59 games for the Royals before the postseason, Zobrist had 66 hits, 23 RBIs, and scored 37 runs. He went hitless in only 18 games. To Yost's point, Zobrist played second base, third base, and the corner outfield spots. He solidified his spot, though, at second base after Omar Infante suffered an oblique strain in September.

"Zo's a phenomenal guy, a phenomenal player," Mike Moustakas told *USA TODAY* during the postseason. "He's the guy that's out there playing hard every single day, energetic, fired up when things are going good, letting everybody know when things aren't. He's been a huge addition to what we do here." ∎

A versatile position player and clutch hitter, Ben Zobrist drives in Alcides Escobar during Game 3 of the American League Championship Series.

2
SS

Alcides Escobar

6
OF

Lorenzo Cain

Trading Away Greinke Netted Royals Valuable Assets

Zack Greinke had been a great pitcher for the Royals, a Cy Young Award-winning dominating pitcher, but, like everyone who plays this game, he wanted to play on a championship-caliber team. The Royals weren't quite at that point in 2010 when Greinke suggested to general manager Dayton Moore that the club trade some of its top minor league prospects for major league players.

Feeling a need for an impact centerfielder and an upgrade at either shortstop or second base, Moore opened trade discussions to help get Greinke to a contender. The perfect suitor ended up being the Milwaukee Brewers, who had an up-and-coming centerfielder named Lorenzo Cain, who split time in 2010 between Double A, Triple A, and the majors. Originally, the Brewers were going to send Cain and pitcher Jake Odorizzi to Kansas City in exchange for Greinke. Moore really wanted Milwaukee shortstop Alcides Escobar as part of the deal, though, so he offered to add Yuniesky Betancourt in exchange for Escobar.

"I liked Escobar and Cain mainly for their speed and defense," Moore said. "The Brewers were giving up players of the future in exchange for a front-line starter and Cy Young award winner who could help them get back to the playoffs."

From Day One in 2011, Escobar became Kansas City's shortstop and he's started nearly every game since.

His .980 fielding percentage in 2015 equals his career best. Also in 2015, he was an A.L. All-Star for the first time. Offensively, Escobar has been up and down during his five seasons with the Royals. Yet in spite of his .257 batting average, 26 walks, and relatively low .293 on-base percentage in 2015, something magical happened to the Royals when Escobar hit in the lead-off spot. They won—a lot.

"Statistically speaking it doesn't make any sense," said Royals manager Ned Yost, who knew Escobar and Cain from his days managing Milwaukee. "But it works. It works. We find ways to win baseball games. We were 32 games over .500 with him in the leadoff,

Lorenzo Cain (left) and Alcides Escobar slap hands at home plate after Cain's home run against the Chicago White Sox on April 8. Cain and Escobar were obtained from the Brewers in a December 2010 trade that sent starter Zack Greinke to Milwaukee.

and I decided to move him down, and we went 10–18. So as soon as I put him back in, the last seven games he led off to end the season we won all seven of them, at a time we needed to win them to accomplish our home-field advantage goal.

"It's just the chemistry of the lineup somehow that is kind of unexplainable to me how it works and why it works, but it does."

Even though everyone knows he's likely swinging at the first pitch, teams kept starting him off with fastballs, and he kept hitting them. During the ALCS he set a major-league record by leading off his team's half of the first with a hit in four consecutive postseason games. Then he led off the bottom of the first in Game 1 of the World Series with an inside-the-park home run against Matt Harvey and the New York Mets—on the first pitch, of course. Escobar became the first player to hit an inside-the-park homer in the World Series since 1929.

Escobar was impressive enough during the ALCS that he was the series' MVP.

"For me it's a surprise," Escobar said of the award. "I know I'm playing really good, and my team is playing really good. Together we play. And when I heard the news, I was so happy for that."

Yost was thrilled for him, too.

"I used to bring Esky to big league spring training when he was in A ball because I loved to watch him play," Yost said. "For him to get the MVP this year is very satisfying to me. I've always known he was an MVP type of player in these type of situations. I'm excited for him."

Coincidentally, the Royals player who won the 2014 ALCS MVP award? Lorenzo Cain.

Cain, who's become known for his infectious smile and the way he's tormented on Instagram by his close friend Salvador Perez, had a slower route to Kansas City than Escobar. Cain spent the majority of 2011 at Triple A

Alcides Escobar scores the winning run in Game 1 of the World Series, tagging from third on a sacrifice fly by Eric Hosmer.

Omaha and didn't make the full transition to the major leagues until 2012. That's understandable, though, for the latest bloomer of all late bloomers.

"Many people felt he was major league ready," Moore wrote in his book *More Than a Season*. "He didn't complain at all, but I could tell he wasn't sure what to think of us, and we had to build that relationship."

Cain didn't play organized baseball until he was 16—when he was a freshman in high school—after he failed to make the Madison County High School (Florida) basketball team. But there he was, a little more than a decade later, on a stage in the middle of the field at Kauffman Stadium, accepting the ALCS MVP award.

"To see him on that stage throughout the postseason and to know what he meant to our team in 2014 was incredible," Moore said. "I was happy and proud for him in his personal growth as a player and as a man."

Cain's growth as a player continued in the 2015 season, which was his best offensive season thus far in his career. During the regular season, he had career highs in batting average (.307), hits (169), runs (101), doubles (34), triples (six), home runs (16), RBIs (72), walks (37), and a tie for stolen bases (28).

Zack Greinke remains one of the top pitchers in the majors, but his willingness to be traded, Moore's patience, and Yost's history managing Milwaukee all helped give the Royals two key components—Escobar and Cain—to the club's recent success.

"They needed time to develop and grow," Yost said before Game 1 of the 2015 World Series. "Both of those kids were about as skinny as a broomstick. You could tell that they had good actions and good eyes, they were very athletic, and—once they filled out and developed—that they had a chance to be really, really good players. And they both have turned into that." ■

Lorenzo Cain receives high-fives from teammates after scoring a run in a September 2015 game against Seattle. Cain, who did not begin playing basketball until age 16, reached career highs in batting average (.307), hits (169), runs (101), doubles (34), triples (six), home runs (16), RBIs (72), and walks (37) in 2015.

Royals Clinch AL Central

K.C. Wins its Division for the First Time Since 1985

The 2015 Royals weren't expected to do much. Most of the so-called experts felt Kansas City's 2014 postseason run was either a fluke or the club didn't do anything to get better in 2015.

ESPN polled its 88 experts, and only three picked the Royals to win the American League Central. Not one picked them to be in the World Series. Only one of CBS Sports' five experts picked the Royals to win the division; one picked them to win a wild-card spot. Neither thought they'd win the league. None of *Sports Illustrated's* six experts nor Yahoo Sports' five picked the Royals to reach the postseason, let alone win the division.

And, yet, there they were, at Kauffman Stadium on September 24, facing the Seattle Mariners (a team many thought would be in the World Series) with a magic number of two and a chance to become the first team to clinch a division in Major League Baseball.

As far as seasons and great Royals teams are concerned, the 2015 season was among the best. Kansas City won its first seven games and didn't slow down throughout the first five months. The Royals never dipped below second place and even in second place they never were more than one game back. After beating the Minnesota Twins on June 9 and seeing their record at 10 games above .500 (33–23), the Royals remained in first in the AL Central for the rest of the season. On August 19 they led the division by 14½ games. It was reminiscent of 1980, when the Royals took over first place in the AL West in May and had a double-digit lead in the standings throughout the last two months.

The Royals didn't look mortal in 2015 until September. They finished the month with an 11–17 record, which was the first time they didn't finish above .500 during a month since going 12–13 in July 2014, a span of seven regular-season months.

But that didn't matter at 10:30 PM on September 24, 2015. Behind a home run and a double by both Eric Hosmer and Mike Moustakas, who had three hits—as did Alex Rios, not to mention the pitching of Johnny Cueto, the Royals overcame a 3–2 deficit in the fifth inning en route to a 10–4 win over the Mariners, just moments after Cleveland beat Minnesota 6–3. The Royals win, coupled with the Twins loss, sealed the divison championship for Kansas City. It's the first time the Royals have won the Central division, and it's the club's first division title since winning the AL West in 1985.

"When I woke up this morning, I had a great feeling we would win it," Royals manager Ned Yost said.

Eric Hosmer embraces third-base coach Mike Jirschele after the Royals clinch their first division title since 1985.

"When I looked up and saw that Cleveland had scored six runs, I knew that this was going to be our night."

With the game tied at 1–1 in the bottom of the second inning, Moustakas gave the Royals a 2–1 lead with a leadoff homer to right off Seattle starter James Paxton.

Cueto got shaky in the fourth, though, and saw the small lead evaporate. A lead-off single by Robinson Cano and back-to-back doubles by Seth Smith and Mark Trumbo gave the Mariners a 3–2 lead.

After Hosmer tied the game with a home run in the fifth, the Royals' offense—as they are prone to do-ing—scored runs in bunches. Kansas City added two more runs in both the sixth and seventh innings and then three in the eighth.

Besides big nights for Hosmer, Moustakas, and Rios, Ben Zobrist had two doubles and scored three runs, and Lorenzo Cain had two hits, two RBIs, and scored a run.

In spite of the shaky fourth, Cueto went seven innings for Kansas City, giving up seven hits and three runs. He walked two and struck out five, as his record went to 10–12 on the season.

Ryan Madson pitched the eighth. With Kansas City's lead at 10–3, Wade Davis pitched the ninth for the Royals. He gave up a leadoff homer to Logan Morrison and walked Brad Miller before striking out the next two Mariners—Shawn O'Malley and Ketel Marte—and inducing a ground-out by Kyle Seager.

"I've felt all along we would win this division. I've got my eyes on a much bigger prize," Yost said. "This is the first step of it." ■

Eric Hosmer hits a solo shot—his 16th home run of the season—in the fifth inning of the 10-4 victory.

17

PITCHER

Wade Davis

Last Year's Superlative Set-Up Man Becomes Dominant Closer in '15

Wade Davis delivered one of the most memorable relief outings in team history.

It was Game 6 of the American League Championship Series against the Toronto Blue Jays, and the contest was tied in the eighth inning after Ryan Madson gave up a two-run home run to Jose Bautista and then walked Edwin Encarnacion. Royals manager Ned Yost called on Davis.

Davis not only got the last two outs of the eighth inning, but also had to stay warm through a 45-minute rain delay before returning for the ninth. The Royals had been uncertain about whether he should continue—an hour would pass between his last pitch in the eighth inning and his first pitch in the ninth—but they allowed Davis to make the call.

Kansas City had taken a 4–3 lead in the bottom of the eighth when Lorenzo Cain scored from first on a single. Not surprisingly, Davis wanted to be on the mound.

"As long as I felt loose," Davis said afterwards, "I felt I was coming back out, especially after we scored."

As Yost pointed out after the game, injured closer Greg Holland, who anchored the bullpen during Kansas City's postseason run in 2014 and for most of the 2015 season, told Yost to let Davis loose.

"Don't worry about nothing," Holland said. "Wade wants to go to the World Series."

Davis did not look as sharp in the ninth, allowing a hit to the first batter and a walk to the second. A few steals later, Davis faced a situation that included runners at second and third and one out. One strikeout later Davis faced Josh Donaldson, whom many expected to be named the American League MVP.

Davis won the at-bat, inducing a ground-out to Mike Moustakas at third, and the Royals won the game and advanced to the World Series for the second straight season.

"Unbelievable," Moustakas said. "That's so tough to do. Wade's been phenomenal, and for him to come back and do that after a delay—unreal."

The game cemented Davis' legacy with the Royals, showcasing all the same elements that allowed him to record a regular season ERA of 0.94 in 69 appearances

Closer Wade Davis rejoices after putting away the Toronto Blue Jays in Game 6 despite pitching through a lengthy rain delay.

in 2015, a slight improvement over his 1.00 ERA during 71 outings in 2014. During 2014 Davis didn't allow a run for 20 appearances and didn't give up an extra-base hit for 43 appearances.

Davis upped his performance even as he shifted late in the season to a different role, going from eighth inning set-up man to ninth inning closer. Holland had struggled throughout the season due to elbow issues that would eventually require Tommy John surgery, so the Royals eventually shut him down and tabbed Davis to replace him.

Oakland A's catcher Stephen Vogt was a teammate of Davis when both played for the Tampa Bay Rays, and Vogt spoke with the *New York Times* in July—when Davis would pitch in his first All-Star Game—about what made Davis so effective.

"His stuff just explodes out of his hand," Vogt said. "He's just got such a good mix. You don't know what's coming. With a lot of relievers, their stuff is so good, but it's fastball or wipeout slider. With him he can throw you a cutter, he can throw you a 2–0 curveball for a strike, he can throw you a four-seam fastball. You just never know. You can't sit on anything because he's got 98."

Davis has starter's stuff with a closer's mentality.

When the Royals acquired him following the 2012 season, little hubbub ensued. The centerpiece of the trade was starting pitcher James Shields, a former All-Star who had logged six straight seasons of 200-plus innings. By comparison Davis had a 4.22 ERA over 64 starts in parts of three seasons for the Rays and had spent the 2012 season in the bullpen. Many saw him as an add-on to the trade. General manager Dayton Moore has long contended that wasn't the case; the Royals felt Davis could make an impact for Kansas City.

"We felt that he could start," Moore said. "He'd successfully started in the past, and we needed a starter. In 2012 he was dominant in the bullpen, so we knew that if it didn't work out as a starter, he could be a dominant reliever."

Wade Davis delivers a pitch during the ninth inning of an 8–6 victory against the Boston Red Sox in which he recorded his 11th save.

The Royals planned to start Davis, and they did for a while. Davis started 24 games in 2013. Between those starts and seven relief appearances, he turned in a 5.32 ERA.

Then came spring training in 2014, when reliever Luke Hochevar, who was going to be a set-up man for Holland, hurt his elbow, requiring Tommy John surgery.

"As Ned and I discussed it, we decided that our best option would be moving Wade Davis into Hoch's spot," Moore wrote in his book, *More Than a Season*. "No one —and I mean no one—could've predicted how dominant Wade would be."

And that trend has continued, whether he's setting up for Holland or striking out the league MVP in the clinching game of the American League Championship Series.

"He just makes hitters look like complete fools," Hochevar told the *Kansas City Star* in July. "He can do whatever he wants." ■

Top: Closer Wade Davis saves his first game of the postseason in Game 2 of the American League Division Series. Opposite: During an August 6, 2015 game, Davis throws during the eighth inning, the frame he used to dominate as the Royals' set-up man.

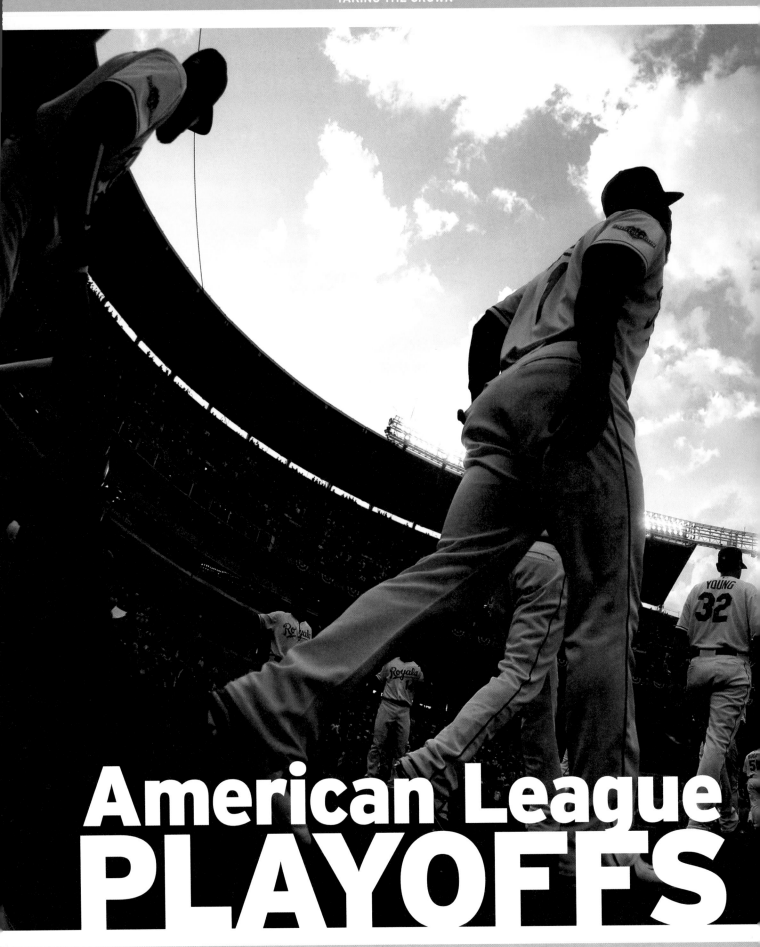

American League
PLAYOFFS

The Royals take the field at Kauffman Stadium prior to Game 1 of the American League Division Series against the Houston Astros.

AMERICAN LEAGUE DIVISION SERIES: GAME 1

OCTOBER 8, 2015 | ASTROS 5, ROYALS 2

In the Hole

Astros Take Early Lead Against Ventura in Rain-Delayed Opener

As the late Yogi Berra said, "It's déjà vu all over again." A young team, fresh off a surprising wild-card win, waltzed in and beat the favorites in Game 1 of the American League Division Series.

Only, this time, it was the Houston Astros opening Kansas City Royals 2015 postseason by going into Kauffman Stadium and taking care of the favored Royals 5–2 in the best-of-five series. In 2014 it was the Royals beating the Los Angeles Angels of Anaheim.

Kansas City starting pitcher Yordano Ventura, who had gone 9–1 during the last two-plus months of the regular season, dating back to a win on July 26 over Houston, was less than sharp during his first two innings against the Astros this time around.

Ventura gave up three runs on four hits and a walk in the first two innings. Two of those runs came in the first. After the first three Astros—Jose Altuve, George Springer, and Carlos Correa—reached base, Houston took an early 2–0 lead on ground-outs by Colby Rasmus and Evan Gattis.

"There's no doubt the first inning set the tone and gave our team a little bit of an exhale," said Houston manager A.J. Hinch. "To put up five quality at-bats in the first inning and get two runs, that's sort of announcing your presence there. I loved how our team came out and did that."

The Astros took a 3–0 lead in the top of the second after Altuve, who had three hits in the game, lined a two-out single to right that scored Jake Marisnick, who doubled a batter earlier.

Kansas City got on the board in the bottom of the second on a lead-off home run to right by Kendrys Morales against Houston starter Collin McHugh, who allowed only five Royals to reach base in six innings.

Immediately after the final out of the second inning, though, rain halted play for 49 minutes. Coming out of the rain delay, Yost decided to replace Ventura with Chris Young, while Hinch decided to stick with McHugh.

"He was just settling in when it started to rain," Yost said of Ventura. "He got hurt with his curveball the first inning, two pitches that were up in the zone a little bit. But besides that, he did a nice job of kind

Pitcher Chris Young, who replaced Yordano Ventura following a rain delay, throws during the third inning.

of limiting the damage there. Could have been worse. I just felt like he was starting to get in his rhythm when the rain came. [The delay] was pushing 60 minutes there. So we made the decision to go with Chris Young, and he came in and did a nice job for us."

Indeed. Young, who was pitching unexpectedly only three days after the funeral for his father, Charles, came in after the rain delay and struck out the first six Astros he faced (seven overall). He went on to give up only one hit and two walks in four innings.

"Chris has been throwing the ball so well for us lately, it gave us confidence to go out in the third inning to hold the score," Yost said. "[He] got us into the sixth inning in the game, and that's what you're looking for."

In spite of Ventura's shaky start, pitching wasn't the issue for the Royals; it was getting the offense going against McHugh, a 19-game winner during the regular season. Kansas City's only other run came in the fourth inning, when Morales launched his second homer of the game and cut the Astros' lead to 3–2.

"We could not get any type of rally going," Yost said. "We got little mini-rallies going, but we couldn't sustain them. He just made pitches and kept us off balance with his off-speed stuff, commanded his ball well, and after sitting for an hour, my hope was maybe he'd stiffen up a little bit. But, no, he came back just as sharp as he was in the first two innings."

The Astros added an insurance run in the eighth inning when Colby Rasmus lined a solo home run to right-center field against Ryan Madson. ■

Designated hitter Kendrys Morales celebrates with teammates after hitting a solo home run in the second inning of Game 1.

AMERICAN LEAGUE DIVISION SERIES: GAME 2
OCTOBER 9, 2015 | **ROYALS 5, ASTROS 4**

Late Bloomers

Royals Take First Lead in Series in Seventh Inning

The Kansas City Royals grabbed their first lead of the 2015 postseason in the bottom of the seventh inning of Game 2 en route to a 5–4 win against the Houston Astros, evening the five-game series at one game apiece. Kansas City had trailed for 16 innings, including the entirety of Game 1.

After tying Game 2 at 4–4 with two runs in the bottom of the sixth, the Royals took the lead in the seventh. Facing relief pitcher Will Harris, Alcides Escobar led off the inning with a triple to center field. The next batter, Ben Zobrist, singled to left, scoring Escobar and giving Kansas City a 5–4 lead.

At that point Royals manager Ned Yost could breathe a little easier with Ryan Madson and Wade Davis sitting in the bullpen ready to replace Kelvin Herrera. Madson retired the Astros in order, getting Evan Gattis to ground out, and then striking out Luis Valbuena and Chris Carter.

The ninth didn't go quite as smoothly for Davis, who struck out pinch-hitter Jed Lowrie but then walked pinch-hitter Preston Tucker. Carlos Gomez, whom the Astros acquired from Milwaukee in a July trade, came in to pinch run for Tucker. Davis isn't exactly known for his pick-off move, but in an effort to keep Gomez close to the base, he made a quick throw to first. Eric Hosmer snatched the bad throw from Davis and applied the tag on a diving Gomez, who was safe, according to first base umpire Mike Everitt. The Royals challenged the call, however, and it was overturned.

"Wade threw it to the perfect spot," Hosmer said. "I felt [Gomez's] arm graze my glove just a little bit. I wasn't really sure if we got him or not, but I wanted to give the boys in the video room a chance to check."

Houston's lead-off batter, Jose Altuve, who was hitless in four at-bats after getting three in Game 1, grounded out to Mike Moustakas, giving the Royals a split at home.

The win didn't come easily, though, for the Royals after a shaky start by starting pitcher Johnny Cueto. For a second consecutive game, the Astros jumped ahead early. After getting Altuve to fly out to Lorenzo Cain, Cueto walked George Springer. Two batters and one out later, Colby Rasmus doubled to right, giving Houston a 1–0 lead. In the second the Astros loaded

Alcides Escobar is exuberant after leading off the seventh inning with a triple. He would score to give the Royals their first lead of the series.

the bases before Altuve flied out to Alex Rios. Springer, however, then blooped a two-run single that scored Carter and Jason Castro.

The Royals got one of those runs back in the bottom of the second when Salvador Perez lined a home run to left off Houston starter Scott Kazmir. But the Astros came right back and re-took their three-run lead when Rasmus led off the top of the third with a home run to right. With that, Rasmus had a home run in each of the Astros' three postseason games, starting with Houston's wild-card contest against New York.

Kansas City added a run in the bottom of the third before tying the game in the sixth. Cain roped a one-out double to right against Kazmir. And then after Houston manager A.J. Hinch turned to reliever Oliver Perez, Hosmer singled to center. He eventually went to third after a single by Kendrys Morales and a walk to Mike Moustakas and then scored on a walk to Perez by reliever Josh Fields.

"Once we tied that ballgame up in the sixth inning there, you know that you got Herrera, Madson and you've got Davis," Yost said. "You feel really good about your chances of holding the score right there until you can score.

"Thankfully, we scored in the seventh, got it done there. And Madson came in and was tremendous, and Wade Davis was unbelievable." ∎

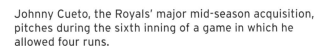

Johnny Cueto, the Royals' major mid-season acquisition, pitches during the sixth inning of a game in which he allowed four runs.

AMERICAN LEAGUE DIVISION SERIES: GAME 3

| OCTOBER 11, 2015 | ASTROS 4, ROYALS 2 |

Losing to Dallas in Houston

Keuchel Thwarts Royals, Allows Just One Run

On paper this was a bad matchup for the Royals. After all Houston Astros pitcher Dallas Keuchel had a perfect home record in 2015. He lived up to the tough billing as the Astros went on to beat the Royals 4–2 and take a two games to one lead in the best-of-five series.

Keuchel, who was 15–0 at Minute Maid Park during the regular season, kept the Royals off balance for the better part of seven innings. The Astros' ace scattered five hits and allowed only one run, a solo home run by Lorenzo Cain on a 10-pitch at-bat in the fourth that gave Kansas City a 1–0 lead.

That's not to say the Royals didn't have their chances. In fact, Kansas City had at least one runner in scoring position in five of Keuchel's seven innings.

"He threw a great game," Royals manager Ned Yost said. "At times with runners in scoring position, we probably swung at some balls that probably wouldn't have been called strikes, but that's what good movement does. That's what he does so well is he changes speeds, he moves location. He moves it in, he moves it out. He speeds it up, he slows it down. I think

he should be the Cy Young winner this year. He's been great, had a phenomenal year."

Yost's starting pitcher, Edinson Volquez, whose consistency early in the year helped keep the Royals in first place throughout the season, matched Keuchel for most of the game. Through the first four innings he faced just two batters more than the minimum. His trouble inning was the fifth, when he walked Luis Valbuena with one out, gave up a double to Chris Carter, and then a two-run single to Jason Castro that put the Astros ahead for good at 2–1.

Carter, though, was far from finished, though. In the bottom of the seventh, with the Astros leading 3–1 after an RBI single by Carlos Gomez an inning earlier, Carter launched a towering lead-off home run off Danny Duffy to left center. Carter gave Houston its first hit of the game, a single off the left-field wall in the third, but he was thrown out by Alex Gordon trying to stretch it into a double.

"Volquez threw unbelievably good," Yost said. "Both pitches that they capitalized on with runners in scoring position were actually great pitches...Both

Edinson Volquez reacts after giving up a two-run single to Astros catcher Jason Castro during the fifth inning of Game 3.

pitches were great pitches, but they found ways to put the ball on the outfield grass. I thought Eddie was throwing the ball great. I thought he was superb today."

The Royals added a run in the ninth inning when Gordon sent a Luke Gregerson pitch over the wall in left center. The loss put the Royals one loss from elimination with one more game in Houston and a potential Game 5 in Kansas City.

"You got to go out and win, we know that," Yost said. "I don't think our mind-set would've changed any if we'd won today. You got to go out and win tomorrow. You don't have much leeway now, but I think our guys are up to the task. Tomorrow will be an exciting day." ■

Above: Starting pitcher Dallas Keuchel throws a pitch during his masterful five-hit, seven-strikeout performance. Opposite: A frustrated Eric Hosmer tosses his helmet after striking out in the fifth inning.

AMERICAN LEAGUE DIVISION SERIES: GAME 4
OCTOBER 12, 2015 | **ROYALS 9, ASTROS 6**

"Keep the Line Moving"

Epic Comeback Ties Series, Sends It Back to K.C.

Besides being in the Royals' favor, there's nothing seemingly spectacular about the final score of 9–6 in Game 4 of the 2015 American League Division Series. But when great Royals postseason games are debated decades from now, this is one that's sure to be near the top of the list, along with the phrase, "Keep the line moving."

The Royals were down to their final six outs of the season with Houston leading by four runs 6–2, heading into the top of the eighth. To make matters worse, Kansas City's Ryan Madson gave up back-to-back home runs to Carlos Correa (his second of the game) and Colby Rasmus in the bottom of the seventh that pushed Houston's lead from 3–2 to 6–2.

But then it happened.

Mike Moustakas, who was batting .143 at the time in the postseason, came in the dugout before the eighth inning and reminded his teammates that it wasn't over.

The G-rated version: "It was just that we're not losing this game. We've worked too hard and we've come too far," Moustakas said.

It wasn't exactly John Belushi's Germans bombing Pearl Harbor speech from Animal House, but it worked. The first five batters in the inning—Alex Rios, Alcides Escobar, Ben Zobrist, Lorenzo Cain, and Eric Hosmer—singled, cutting Houston's lead to 6–4, while the players kept saying to each other in the dugout, "Keep the line moving."

With the bases loaded, the next batter, Kendrys Morales, chopped a ball up the middle against reliever Tony Sipp, but it went off the glove of rookie shortstop Correa for an error. Zobrist and Cain scored, tying the game at 6–6. After Moustakas struck out on a 3–2 pitch for the first out of the inning, catcher Drew Butera, who had replaced Salvador Perez defensively earlier, welcomed pitcher Luke Gregerson into the game by turning a 10-pitch at-bat into a walk.

"Hitting's contagious, and when you see six guys in front of you put together good at-bats and keep the line moving, you don't want to be that guy that just goes up there and swings at it—one, two, three—and heads back to the dugout," Butera said. "That was my plan—

Yordano Ventura, who allowed three runs during Game 4, delivers a pitch during the first inning.

to keep the line moving and get on base."

With the bases loaded once again, Alex Gordon grounded out to second baseman Jose Altuve, which scored Hosmer and gave the Royals an improbable 7–6 lead.

"The thing about this club is that they don't quit; they don't," said Royals manager Ned Yost. "After giving up three runs in the bottom of the seventh, they came in on fire. Our bats were really silent until the eighth inning, but having watched them as much as I've watched them, you know that sooner or later they're going to break out."

After Wade Davis retired the Astros in order in the bottom of the eighth, Kansas City's bats stayed awake. With Zobrist on first after a walk from reliever Josh Fields, Hosmer launched a two-run homer to right-center that gave the Royals a couple insurance runs.

Davis gave up a lead-off single to Correa in the bottom of the ninth before finishing off the Astros by striking out Rasmus, who earlier hit his third home run of the series, and pinch-hitter Preston Tucker and then getting Carlos Gomez to fly out.

"Having Wade come out in the eighth inning and get a six-out save gave us the best opportunity to win that game," Yost said.

This Game 4 comeback was reminiscent of last year's epic comeback against Oakland A's in the wild-card game, when the Royals trailed 7–3 after seven innings before winning in the 12th inning.

Once again, the never-say-die Royals showed their mettle in the postseason. ■

Eric Hosmer caps the Royals' offensive burst with a two-run home run in the ninth inning of Game 4.

Johnny on the Spot

Cueto Retires 19 Straight Batters to Send Astros Home

After the club acquired him from Cincinnati at the trade deadline in July for most of his time with the Royals, Johnny Cueto wasn't the lights-out pitcher many fans expected. But Kansas City got him largely for a situation such as this. And he didn't disappoint.

Cueto was ace-like in his domination of Houston as the Kansas City Royals beat the Houston Astros in decisive fashion in the deciding game of the American League Division Series 7–2 in front of a standing-room-only crowd at Kauffman Stadium.

The win propelled the Royals into a series with Toronto to defend their American League crown.

Cueto allowed only two base runners as he gave up two runs on two hits in eight innings. Besides not allowing a walk, Cueto struck out eight Astros. The only hits and runs came in the top of the second. With two outs Evan Gattis singled. The next batter, Luis Valbuena, homered to right, giving Houston a 2–0 lead. Cueto responded by retiring the next 19 batters.

"He was unbelievably good," Royals manager Ned Yost said of Cueto. "He didn't make a bad pitch all night. That pitch that Valbuena hit was a good pitch."

Cueto wasn't just "unbelievably good," he was historically good. He was the first American League pitcher to record 19 consecutive outs since Don Larsen's perfect game in the 1956 World Series. He became the sixth pitcher to allow no more than two runners in a postseason start that went at least eight innings. The most recent came in 2010, when Roy Halladay no-hit Cincinnati. He also became the fifth pitcher with at least eight strikeouts and no walks in a winner-take-all postseason game.

It took a few innings, but Kansas City's offense helped Cueto. Although the Royals haven't shown off their speed much in the postseason, it was on display in the fourth for the team's first run of the game. With Lorenzo Cain at first base, Eric Hosmer blooped a single to center. Cain, running on the pitch—and never slowing down—scored from first as center fielder Carlos Gomez fell down on the play.

Shortstop Alcides Escobar ignited the Royals during Game 5 from his traditional leadoff spot.

The Royals then tied it and went ahead for good in the fifth inning. Houston starter Collin McHugh, who got the win in Game 1, hit Salvador Perez, leading off the fifth and then gave up a ground-rule double to Alex Gordon. That forced Houston manager A.J. Hinch to go to his bullpen and pull out Mike Fiers. With runners on second and third and no outs, Alex Rios greeted Fiers with a two-run double to left. Two batters late, Ben Zobrist hit a sacrifice fly to right, scoring Rios from third and giving the Royals a 4–2 lead.

"We felt really good at that point because we felt we were at a point in the game where we could involve our bullpen if we needed it," Yost said. "But Johnny was still throwing the ball extremely well. So we felt like at that point we were in really, really good shape."

Kendrys Morales added a three-run home run to center in the bottom of the eighth that gave the Royals the decisive 7–2 lead.

Even though Cueto still looked sharp and had a five-run lead, Yost brought in Wade Davis, who finished off the Astros in order in the ninth.

But it all started with Cueto, who was historically good in the biggest game thus far of the postseason for Kansas City.

"He knew the magnitude of this game, I think we all did, and he came out from the first pitch, just had everything going," Yost said. "He was fantastic." ■

Starting pitcher Johnny Cueto throws during the triumphant Game 5, in which he retired the last 19 Astros batters.

Pitching Gem

Volquez Shuts Down Jays' Bats, Allows Just Two Hits

The Royals had a five-game dogfight with Houston. They expected the same—if not more—from the Toronto Blue Jays, one of the hottest teams in baseball during the second half of the season. They certainly didn't get it in Game 1 of the American League Championship Series, as Kansas City cruised for the first time during this postseason 5–0 over the Blue Jays at Kauffman Stadium.

Starting pitcher Edinson Volquez picked up where Johnny Cueto left off two days earlier. Volquez threw six shutout innings, allowing two hits, while walking four and striking out five. The only two times the Blue Jays got into scoring position against Volquez were in the third and sixth innings. In the third Kevin Pillar led off with a walk and was sacrificed to second by Ryan Goins. But then Volquez got Ben Revere to fly out and Josh Donaldson to ground out. Then in the sixth, Volquez walked the first two batters of the inning, Donaldson and Jose Bautista, but then retired the next three Blue Jays, including strikeouts by Edwin Encarnacion and Troy Tulowitzki.

"One more guy got on, and we were going to go get him," Royals manager Ned Yost said of whether he considered taking out Volquez in the sixth with Kelvin Herrera warming up in the bullpen. "Eddie was superb today, had everything going on, had his great fastball, locating well, really good curveball, really nice change-ups, on the attack from the first inning on. At that point [in the sixth inning], we still liked his stuff. But if he lost that last hitter, we were going to get Kel."

As Volquez worked through that 37-pitch sixth inning, he began to get encouragement from the standing-room only home crowd, as they began chanting, "Eddie! Eddie! Eddie!"

"Hearing that from the fans, it's a lot of energy. They gave me more energy to pitch the way I pitched in that inning," he said. "And that was great to see all those fans there. It was a long inning, but I was happy to stay under control and make a lot of good pitches to get out from that inning. And the key for that inning, I think, is don't panic."

After Volquez worked out of the sixth, Herrera

Edinson Volquez celebrates after striking out Blue Jays shortstop Troy Tulowitzki to cap his six scoreless innings.

pitched a perfect seventh, and Ryan Madson pitched the eighth. By that point the Royals held a 3–0 lead against Toronto starter Marco Estrada. Kansas City scored its first two runs of the game in the third inning. Alex Gordon led off the inning with a double and then scored on a double by Alcides Escobar. Ben Zobrist grounded out, which moved Escobar to third. He scored on a base hit by Lorenzo Cain.

The hit by Escobar was his second of the game, following up his double that led off the Kansas City half of the first inning.

"We like Escobar in that one hole because he can make things happen," Yost said. "[He] got a big base hit there to drive in the first run the opposite way. Lorenzo Cain comes up and does the exact same thing. They're all kind of staying within themselves, trying to take advantage of the pitch that's given to them."

In the fourth inning, Salvador Perez homered to center, giving the Royals a 3–0 lead. Kansas City tacked on two more runs in the bottom of the eighth on an RBI double by Eric Hosmer that scored Escobar, who was hit by a pitch, and then Zobrist scored on a sacrifice fly to left by Kendrys Morales.

The extra runs allowed Yost to save closer Wade Davis. Instead, he brought in Luke Hochevar, who missed the 2014 postseason because of an injury suffered during spring training. Hochevar worked around an error by Mike Moustakas that allowed Dioner Navarro to reach base, as the Royals took a 1–0 lead in the series.

"We win the first game, it's going to be big for the team, especially when we play at home," Volquez said. "You don't want to go to Toronto 0–2. And it was good for the team and for the city, I think. Now we've got a couple more games to play. And I hope we can win tomorrow and show up." ∎

Catcher Salvador Perez homers to left-center field during the fourth inning.

Price Choppers

Toronto's Botched Defensive Play Opens Floodgates for Royals

As significant as a three-run home run can be to the outcome of a baseball game, sometimes it's the little moments that can make an opponent unravel and turn momentum in a hurry. Just ask Toronto left-handed pitcher David Price, who gave up a lead-off single to Alcides Escobar in Game 2 of the ALCS, but then retired the next 18 Royals.

But a bloop base hit in the seventh inning led to another monstrous comeback inning for the Royals as they beat the Toronto Blue Jays 6–3 at Kauffman Stadium and headed north of the border with a two games to none lead in the best-of-seven series.

Price was typical Price for six innings. After Escobar's single that led off the home half of the first, Price settled got into a rhythm befitting of a pitcher who went 18–5 with a 2.45 ERA and 225 strikeouts during the regular season. He kept the Kansas City batters uncomfortable en route to seven strikeouts through six innings.

And then it happened.

With Toronto leading 3–0, Ben Zobrist knocked a high pop-up into shallow right field. Second baseman Ryan Goins charged hard after it and appeared to be calling for it. At the last minute, though, he put on the brakes as if right fielder Jose Bautista called him off. Ultimately, the ball plopped between the two players, and Zobrist had a lead-off single.

That opened the floodgates for Kansas City's offense. Lorenzo Cain knocked a single to right, followed by an RBI hit to center by Eric Hosmer that scored Zobrist and moved Cain to third. Kendrys Morales was the first out of the inning as he grounded out to shortstop Troy Tulowitzki, whose only play was to first because Hosmer was in the process of stealing second. So that cut Toronto's lead to 3–2 as Cain scored and Hosmer went to second. Mike Moustakas then tied the game with a single to center and went to second on the throw to home plate. After Price struck out Perez for his eighth strikeout of the afternoon, he gave up an RBI double to Alex Gordon that gave Kansas City its first lead of the game 4–3. That marked the end of Price's day but not the end of the Royals' scoring. Alex Rios greeted reliever Aaron Sanchez with a single to center that scored Gordon.

"You knew, over the course of the game, that we were going to mount some kind of challenge there," said

Lorenzo Cain celebrates his seventh-inning single—part of a five-run Royals rally.

106

manager Ned Yost. "The key to that whole inning, believe it or not, was Hosmer stealing second base because that was a double-play ball. That kept the inning going and allowed us to get to a point where we could score five runs. That was huge."

Although they didn't need it, the Royals extended their lead to 5–3 with a run in the eighth. Toronto manager John Gibbons used three pitchers in what could've been another disastrous inning for the Blue Jays. Toronto pitchers issued three walks and a run-scoring single by Moustakas but limited the damage.

Yordano Ventura started for Kansas City, and gave up eight hits, two walks, and three runs, and struck out six in five and one-third innings. The three runs all came in the sixth inning. After giving up a lead-off hit to Josh Donaldson and then walking Bautista, Ventura gave up an RBI single to Edwin Encarnacion that made it a 2–0 game. Ventura then struck out Chris Colabello for the first out of the inning before an RBI double by Tulowitzki and a walk to Russell Martin. With the bases loaded and one out, Yost turned to Luke Hochevar. The first batter, Kevin Pillar popped out to Zobrist, and Goins grounded out to Hosmer, ending the inning with Toronto leading 3–0.

"[There are] two or three things that you can look at that really helped us win that game, and Hoch's contribution is one of them," Yost said. "They're a hit away from breaking that game open at 5–0. If it's 3–0, you still feel like you've got a shot to mount an attack. At 5–0 it's a little more daunting because you have to score six to win. When Hoch came in and faced a tough hitter in Pillar and got Goins out, then it's like, 'Okay, we're still right in the middle of this game.'"

Danny Duffy, Kelvin Herrera, and Wade Davis closed out the last three innings for the Royals. It wasn't, however, without some nail-biting. In the ninth inning, Davis started the inning by giving up a single and a walk to Pillar and Cliff Pennington, respectively, before striking out Revere and Donaldson and getting Bautista to fly out to right, leaving Kansas City a two games to none lead. ■

Eric Hosmer scores in the seventh inning to tie Game 2, which the Royals went on to win 6–3.

AMERICAN LEAGUE CHAMPIONSHIP SERIES: GAME 3
OCTOBER 19, 2015 | **BLUE JAYS 11, ROYALS 8**

Jays Pound Cueto

Royals' Late Comeback Falls Short Against Toronto's Big Bats

In one of the most significant starts of his career, with a Kansas City Royals team poised to reach the World Series and with his future earnings as a free agent hanging in the balance, Johnny Cueto turned in one of his worst performances ever.

Cueto allowed eight earned runs—the first time he had done so since 2010—in just two innings in the 11–8 loss to the Toronto Blue Jays in Game 3 of the ALCS.

"He couldn't command the ball down," Royals manager Ned Yost said of Cueto's performance after the game. "He was up all night long, just really struggled with his command, got his pitch count up and just couldn't make an adjustment."

It was so bad that when Cueto, one of the marquee names on the market at the trade deadline, was pulled from the game, fans in Toronto began chanting, "We want Cueto!"

Five days earlier, in Game 5 of the ALDS against the Houston Astros, Cueto had allowed only two earned runs in eight innings.

Against the Blue Jays, however, in Game 3, he looked rattled early on, even though he went out with a lead after his mates notched a run in the first inning on a Ben Zobrist ground out that scored Alcides Escobar, who had led off the game with a triple.

In the second inning Toronto took the lead on a two-run single by Ryan Goins. Another single, this one by Josh Donaldson, scored another run, and the Blue Jays led 3–1.

"You kind of hope he can find a way to make an adjustment," Yost said of Cueto. "He's just up, up, up, up, up. And you're hoping somewhere, at the two-inning mark, you're just hoping that he can make that adjustment. Tonight he just couldn't."

Kansas City chipped the lead to 3–2 in the top of the third, when Eric Hosmer scored Zobrist by grounding into a fielder's choice at first base.

In the bottom of the third inning, Cueto unraveled. Edwin Encarnacion singled, Chris Colabello walked, and Troy Tulowitzki smashed a home run that brought the score to 6–2. Cueto's woes continued. He walked Russell Martin, and Kevin Pillar scored Martin with a

Pitcher Johnny Cueto walks off the mound after a disappointing performance in which he lasted only two innings and allowed eight runs.

double. With the score 7–2, Yost gave Cueto the hook.

Kris Medlen relieved Cueto, but with Pillar on base, he surrendered a home run to Donaldson, making the game 9–2 at the end of the third inning.

The Royals began their comeback attempt in the fifth inning, when Escobar led off with a single, and Zobrist followed him with a double. A wild pitch allowed Escobar to score, and Zobrist to move to third. Mike Moustakas would eventually single in Zobrist, cutting Toronto's lead to 9–4.

Medlen, however, then allowed another home run. Goins hit this one, and it gave the Blue Jays a six-run advantage in the fifth inning. Jose Bautista seemingly put the game out of reach at 11–4 with an RBI single in the eighth.

The Royals—as the Royals have been known to do—put together another rally, this time in the ninth with Escobar and Zobrist both managing to get on base at the beginning of the inning—Escobar via an infield single and Zobrist with a double. The next batter, Lorenzo Cain, lifted a sacrifice fly that brought in Escobar, and a single by Hosmer scored Zobrist. Kendrys Morales put two more runs on the board when he homered with Hosmer on first.

That was as close as the Royals would get, as they ultimately lost 11–8.

"I was proud with our offense tonight the way they swung the bats, all night long," Yost said. "We were down big there, going into the ninth inning, but they didn't quit. They put a four-run on the spot. Eight runs should be enough to win a ballgame, but tonight it wasn't."

And, the late rally was one more example of what the team proved again and again in the 2015 postseason: few leads would be safe against Kansas City. ■

Right fielder Alex Rios makes a diving catch to snare Justin Smoak's fly ball during the eighth inning of Game 3.

AMERICAN LEAGUE CHAMPIONSHIP SERIES: GAME 4
OCTOBER 20, 2015 | **ROYALS 14, BLUE JAYS 2**

No White Knuckler for K.C.

Royals Get to Jays' Starting Pitcher Early and Often

The Kansas City Royals offense found another gear in Game 4 of the ALCS. The Toronto Blue Jays entered the series renowned for their power hitters, but one night after scoring 11 runs against the Royals, Toronto could not even come close to matching Kansas City in Game 4 as the Royals won 14–2.

The Royals chased Toronto starting pitcher R.A. Dickey after only one and two-third innings. The troubles for the 40-year-old knuckleballer began almost instantly. He did not record an out in the first inning until Kansas City had scored three runs.

Ben Zobrist put the Royals on the board with a home run that also scored Alcides Escobar, who got on base with a bunt single. Lorenzo Cain became the third runner to score after he walked, stole second base, moved to third on a single by Eric Hosmer, and crossed home plate on a passed ball. Mike Moustakas scored Hosmer with a sacrifice fly, and the Royals led 4–0.

Alex Rios stretched that lead to 5–0 with a solo homer, but the Blue Jays began to mount a comeback.

In the bottom of the third, Josh Donaldson scored Ryan Goins with a ground-rule double, and Ben Revere scored on a ground out by Jose Bautista.

That would end up being all the offense Toronto could muster that day. The Royals had barely gotten started.

Reliever LaTroy Hawkins entered the game in the seventh and he did not record an out. Instead he walked Salvador Perez and gave up singles to Alex Gordon and Rios. For Rios, a former Blue Jays player who struggled through an injury and the chicken pox during the 2015 season, it was a perfect 3-for-3 day at the plate, including the home run.

"I felt that Alex [Rios] was going to have a great day today," said manager Ned Yost. "I don't know why I felt it, but I did…You feel really good because you know how hard Alex has worked to get to this point this year."

Ryan Tepera replaced Hawkins and he struggled as much as his predecessor did. Perez scored on a sacrifice fly by Escobar, and Gordon scored on a wild pitch. Paulo Orlando, running for Rios, scored on a single by Cain. Zobrist, who had walked, made it across the plate

Ben Zobrist, the second batter of Game 4, celebrates his two-run home run in the first inning against Blue Jays starter R.A. Dickey.

on a sacrifice fly by Hosmer. Thus the 5–2 advantage for the Royals quickly jumped out to 9–2.

Kansas City tacked on three more runs in the eighth, when Perez scored on a sacrifice fly by Escobar, and Gordon and Orlando scored on a single by Cain.

The Royals were impressive enough offensively—and there was enough time left in this series—that Toronto manager John Gibbons turned to infielder Cliff Pennington to pitch in the ninth. He proceeded to give up a single to Orlando and then a two-run single to Escobar, which increased Kansas City's lead to 14–2.

"The offense did a really good job," Hosmer said. "Esky and Zoby continue to set the tone for us at the top of the lineup. We had some good situational hitting today. Anytime we had guys on base, we were moving guys over and cashing in. Against a team like [Toronto], especially in their park, you got to capitalize on those add-on runs as much as you can."

As good as the Royals were offensively, they got great production from their pitchers, too, beginning with starting pitcher Chris Young—who allowed just two earned runs in four and two-third innings—and from the bevy of relievers that followed him.

Luke Hochevar relieved Young and pitched a scoreless one and one-third innings. Ten of his 12 pitches were strikes. Ryan Madson followed Hochevar and notched a pair of strikeouts. Ten of his 15 pitches were strikes. Kelvin Herrera needed just 11 pitches—and eight strikes—in his scoreless inning, and Franklin Morales topped off the display with a scoreless inning of his own. He threw eight of his 14 pitches for strikes.

The 14 runs Kansas City scored in Game 4 were the second-most the Royals had racked up all season. Nine players had hits, and five had more than one hit. The lineup was 8-for-11 with runners in scoring position. ∎

Lorenzo Cain slides past Blue Jays starting pitcher R.A. Dickey to score on a passed ball during the first inning in Game 4.

AMERICAN LEAGUE CHAMPIONSHIP SERIES: GAME 5

OCTOBER 21, 2015 | **BLUE JAYS 7, ROYALS 1**

Royals Bats Go Silent

Sal Perez's Solo HR Represents K.C.'s Only Offensive Output

The Toronto Blue Jays survived the threat of elimination in Game 5 of the ALCS, thanks to a gem from starting pitcher Marco Estrada, who allowed just one run and three hits in seven and two-third innings. The Toronto offense also clicked, helping the Blue Jays secure a 7–1 victory, one day after the Royals had overwhelmed them 14–2.

In Game 5, the Royals had no answer for Estrada, who faced the minimum through 20 batters and struck out five. In terms of earned runs allowed and innings pitched, it was his strongest postseason performance ever.

It was a far cry from the Estrada who gave up three runs on six hits in five and one-third innings in Game 1 of this series.

"Today he was absolutely dynamite," Royals manager Ned Yost said of Estrada. "He didn't miss spots. His change-up was fantastic. He just didn't give us anything to hit. …He did a great job of commanding the baseball, executing his pitches, and keeping us off balance."

Kansas City starting pitcher Edinson Volquez did not fare so well. Toronto took a 1–0 lead in the second inning on a solo home run by Chris Colabello, but overall Volquez looked solid until the sixth inning. From there he unraveled rapidly.

Volquez walked Ben Revere and then hit Josh Donaldson with a pitch. He loaded the bases by walking Jose Bautista and then he walked Edwin Encarnacion, which scored Revere and gave the Blue Jays a 2–0 lead.

Kelvin Herrera came in to replace Volquez, but after he struck out Colabello, Herrera surrendered a three-run double to Troy Tulowitzki, and Toronto led 5–0. Herrera ended the inning by striking out the next two batters, but the damage was done.

Though he isn't the flashiest starter, Volquez had been Kansas City's most dependable hurler all season. He was tagged with five earned runs on three hits and four walks.

Toronto's scoring continued after Volquez departed. The Blue Jays added another run in the seventh—against reliever Danny Duffy—when Bautista doubled in Donaldson.

The Royals got their lone run of the day when

Mike Moustakas reacts after striking out against Marco Estrada, who gave up just three hits, during the second inning of Game 5.

Salvador Perez smacked a solo homer in the top of the eighth. Toronto then led 6–1, but the Blue Jays still had some production left in them. Kevin Pillar doubled in Tulowitzki for the final score.

Given the precedent Kansas City set going into Game 5, scoring 33 runs in the first four games of the ALCS, the offensive outage was a bit surprising.

In no other 2015 postseason game had the Royals been limited to a single run. In the ALDS, the Houston Astros had held Kansas City to two runs in Game 1 and Game 3, both of which the Royals lost.

Going into Game 5 of the ALCS, however, putting up runs had not been an issue; the Royals had averaged 8.25 runs per game through the first four matchups of the series.

In Game 5 the only Royals hitters who had any measure of success—against Estrada that measure was one paltry hit each— were lead-off man Alcides Escobar and the trio that comprises the bottom third of the lineup: Perez, Alex Gordon, and Alex Rios.

All game, Kansas City had only one opportunity to hit with runners in scoring position. The Blue Jays had six such chances, though they only converted on two of them. While the Royals could only scrape together four hits in Game 5, Toronto totaled eight, and Tulowitzki, Pillar, and Bautista each had two.

The Royals still have two chances to win one game and the series—and they'll be doing it in the friendly confines of Kauffman Stadium.

"We knew it was going to be a tough series, but after winning the first two games, in reality your goal is to come to Toronto, in kind of a foreign environment, a hostile environment, and at least win one," Yost said. "Now we're going back to a place where we're completely comfortable. That's why home-field was so important to us. We really wanted to play four games in our park. And we're taking a three game-to-two-lead back to where we are comfortable and back to our home fans that support us and are fantastic." ■

Shortstop Alcides Escobar leaps over Edwin Encarnacion to turn a double play during the fourth inning of Game 4.

AMERICAN LEAGUE CHAMPIONSHIP SERIES: GAME 6
OCTOBER 23, 2015 | ROYALS 4, BLUE JAYS 3

Rain-Delayed Gratification

Wade Davis, Clutch Royals Send K.C. Back to World Series

The Kansas City Royals closed out the American League Championship Series with all the drama a television network could dream—the loss of an early lead, the match-up of the game's best closer against the likely league MVP, the complication of a rain delay, and the heart-stopping sprint of a runner going from first to home on a single to score the winning run.

And after all that, with Blue Jays stranded at second and third in the ninth inning, the Royals secured a 4–3 win and the American League championship, winning it back-to-back for the first time in the organization's history.

The Royals came out swinging in Game 6 against Cy Young hopeful David Price. Ben Zobrist homered in the first inning, and Mike Moustakas sent a ball to the standing-room only crowd in right field in the second inning, letting Kansas City enjoy an early 2–0 lead.

In the fourth inning, Toronto's Jose Bautista, who stepped up to the plate while boos hailed on top of him, brought the Blue Jays within 2–1 with a solo homer.

Kansas City gained a little breathing room in the seventh inning when Alex Rios drove in Moustakas with a single and moved the score to 3–1, but any calm would not last long. Bautista drilled another home run in the eighth, and this one was good for two runs.

With the game tied 3–3, Royals manager Ned Yost called on trusty setup-man-turned-closer Wade Davis. Davis got Kansas City out of the eighth with the tie intact.

For Davis to return to the mound in the ninth, however, he would have to weather a 45-minute rain delay—obviously not an ideal situation for a pitcher wanting to stay warm and to stay in rhythm.

The delay did not seem to bother the Kansas City offense, which had become so adept at dramatic comebacks. The group made perhaps its most exciting one to date in the eighth inning, following the delay. Lorenzo Cain walked, and Eric Hosmer drilled a single to right field. As the ball carried toward Bautista, Cain burst away from first base like a rocket and—with the blessing of third-base coach Mike Jirschele, who recognized that Bautista's throw would give Cain the time he needed—steamed all the way to home plate and scored the winning run.

Ben Zobrist points skyward after hitting a 373-foot home run off Blue Jays pitcher David Price to get the Royals on the scoreboard in the first inning.

"It worked because Lorenzo Cain never slowed down," Yost said. "He didn't just take for granted that he was going to third base. And Jirschele knew that in those situations Bautista comes up and fires to second base, and [Jirschele] was waving him all along. It was a huge send by Jirsch."

It also provided some redemption, considering the Royals' last season ended when Alex Gordon was stranded ninety feet away from home plate. After the game some questioned whether they should've sent Gordon home instead of hoping Salvador Perez would drive him home.

Davis sported regular season numbers among the best in the game and without question he was the best reliever in an excellent Kansas City bullpen, but he kept fans guessing for a few harrowing minutes toward the end of the game if he'd be able to seal the win unscathed.

Russell Martin led off the ninth with a single. Dalton Pompey pinch-ran for Martin and in a matter of pitches, stole second base and then third. Kevin Pillar walked and then stole second. The Blue Jays had runners on second and third with one out. Davis worked out of the jam, however, striking out Ben Revere and then inducing a ground-out by Josh Donaldson, whom many believed would be the American League MVP.

"You know what, every once in a while you've got to give credit to the other side," Toronto manager John Gibbons said. "They got to this round like us because they have great pitching. When they turn over the bullpen, you see what you saw tonight."

The Royals had won the pennant for a second straight season and again they had arrived at the World Series with a confidence developed from successful rally after successful rally. Through the first two rounds of the postseason, five of Kansas City's seven wins had been the result of comebacks—four after falling behind initially and another after obtaining the lead and then losing it.

Kansas City players had spoken throughout the season about wanting to prove their 2014 run to the World Series was no fluke, and they certainly proved it in the ALCS.

"I am honored to accept this trophy on behalf of the Kansas City Royals organization—the players, coaches, the front office," said Royals owner David Glass, as he accepted the American League championship trophy on the podium near second base. "But I'm really proud to accept this on behalf of you, the fans. Without you, this would not have been possible. Now let's go finish what we didn't finish last year." ■

The Royals celebrate their dramatic Game 6 victory, returning them to the World Series for the second consecutive season.

Royals owner David Glass looks on as Alcides Escobar kisses his 2-year-old son, Massimiliano, while accepting the ALCS MVP award. Escobar collected 11 hits in 23 at-bats in the series.